The Freeze Drying Handbook

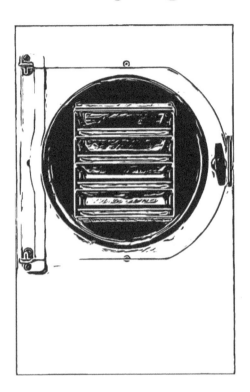

Everything You Need to Know and More!

by

Live. Life. Simple.

Copyright

Legal Notice

The freeze drying information found in this book is for reference only. Information and results will vary greatly from lots of different variables including but not limited to type of foods used, amount of food used, your climate, size of freeze dryer, condition of freeze dryer, age of freeze dryer, software used, vacuum pumps, your ability to follow directions ;) etc.

The best thing that you can do to ensure you get the best possible results from your freeze dryer is to educate yourself, take the knowledge you gain and apply it to your specific situation.

The information in this book is true and complete to the best of our knowledge. The authors and publisher do not assume any liability for the use of any or all the information contained in this book and do not accept responsibility for any loss or damage that may result from the use of instructions or information in this book. All recommendations are made without guarantee. The author reserves the right to make changes to future versions of this book to maintain accuracy.

ISBN: 9798376720110

Dedication

To all my fellow freeze dryers who have shared their wisdom. With your knowledge and contributions, the freeze drying community grows and thrives every day.
Much gratitude as I feel eternally blessed to have such an outstanding community!

The Freeze Drying Handbook

Introduction

My name is Brian and I have been freeze drying since 2017. When I started freeze drying, home freeze drying was in its infancy. The freeze dryers from Harvest Right had been out for a few years, but the machines that predated mine (2017) were very expensive, bulky, inefficient and there were lots of quirks and bugs to be worked out. I had my eye on them for a long time and in 2017, the company really upped their game. The machines were of great quality and the prices had finally come down. My wife bought me a medium freeze dryer for my birthday and little did we know it, it would take us down a whole different life path in the future.

We had been planning from our early 30's to retire at the ripe young age of 40 and we had a very strict plan to do so. Freeze drying would fit right into our plan. We had worked hard for 20 years, lived below our means and reinvested every penny we could and with freeze drying, we could save all of our food (none goes to waste,) and also take advantage of 100% of our garden. We could also take advantage of other peoples' gardens when they had more veggies than they know what to do with at the end of the season. Immediately after I found out I was getting a freeze dryer; I naturally went to the biggest information source on freeze drying. WAIT! I quickly figured out that there was no major source of information for freeze drying. There were a few videos on YouTube and a small Facebook group, but I had so many questions that I wanted answers to. When you are dealing with a whole new technology and an unknown appliance, it's easy for a person to feel overwhelmed!

For some reason, (I still can't figure out why), I decided I was going to take my cheap $50 camera and my new freeze dryer and make a YouTube video on setting up the freeze dryer. Believe it or not, I'm a socially awkward and introverted person but once I got that first video posted and received a few comments on how it had helped someone, I was hooked. I was able to help someone that was in the same position I was in a few weeks prior. They had just purchased a machine that they had no idea how to use and were suffering from what I call "newbie paralysis." You feel like there is so much to know, but don't know where to start.

Enter the Live.Life.Simple YouTube channel. I now have over 300 videos, a Facebook Group, A MeWe group, the www.freezedryingsupplies.com store where we make products that help freeze dryers, an online cookbook www.freezedryingcookbook.com , a hard copy cookbook (with more in the works) and now this book which will probably be followed by many more.

To say that a freeze dryer changed my life sounds like a funny statement. But my wife and I wake up every day with our first thought being something about freeze drying. Ever since that first YouTube comment saying that I had helped someone, I found a new purpose for what I was doing with my life. Really nothing has changed over the years other than we can now help **tens of thousands of freeze dryers all over the world!** Although we are no longer "retired" (it was short lived), we do what we love every day and some would say, "if you do what you love, you never work a day in your life."

I hope to take my knowledge of freeze drying and share it with you in this book and I hope that you can overcome the "newbie paralysis" that I went through. My hope is that this book will be helpful for all freeze dryers, beginners and seasoned experts and be used as a helpful guidebook. If you see something that you already know, you can skip ahead, but you never know, you might just learn something new! I still learn new things almost daily and with more and more people freeze drying, we get new data and a fresh look at things every day.

HAPPY FREEZE DRYING!

Find all our contacts and resources here:

Live.Life.Simple.

https://www.youtube.com/@live.life.simple./videos

Retired at 40's Freeze Drying Group

Retired at 40's Freeze Drying Group

www.freezedryingsupplies.com

www.freezedryingcookbook.com

Avid Armor Vacuum Chamber Sealer
(Use Promo Code LIVELIFESIMPLE for 10% off)
https://avidarmor.com?aff=43

Live. Life. Simple's: Amazon Store
All Our Favorite Products!
https://www.amazon.com/shop/retiredat40

If you are considering purchasing a freeze dryer
Support our community and purchase
through our affiliate link!
https://affiliates.harvestright.com/416.html

Chapter 1

The Many Benefits of Freeze Drying

First and foremost, the fact that you can own a "home use" freeze dryer in and of itself is amazing. Until Harvestright created a home version and now a semi-commercial style freeze dryer, freeze drying was reserved for big corporations. Freeze dried foods that you find in the store are extremely expensive. Why? A commercial freeze dryer costs $100,000's and you are also paying for the knowledge and the experience of the company, and in some cases, how to make an entire freeze dried meal. The following benefits are common for most freeze dryers, but I want to mention that your benefits may be different from my benefits or the next person's. The reason you freeze dry may be different from the reason I freeze dry, which may be different from the reason the next person freeze dries! Whatever your reason is, with a freeze dryer, you will end up with a stash of high quality, high nutrient food that, if executed properly, will store for 25+ years.

The biggest benefit for most freeze dryers is the ability to have a shelf stable food or meal that will last 20, 25 years or even more. Food if stored properly (see food storage 101) without light, moisture and oxygen, can easily last decades. Not only does it last a long time, it's lightweight, easy to make and with the Harvest Right freeze dryer, you can sock away a whole lot of food in a short amount of time. The newest XL size freeze dryer claims that it is capable of freeze drying 5,000 pounds of food per year. To be able to process that amount of food per year at home at the price point that it sells for is also amazing.

Freeze dried food also retains 98% + of its original nutrients, vitamins etc. Cooking food, canning food, dehydrating or freezing can change a food's nutritional value by 50% or more. Just that alone is giving you a food quality that is almost twice as good as the other alternatives. Stack that with the fact that it stores for decades with no refrigeration or maintenance and in most cases tastes identical to when it was fresh. I don't see any other option that even comes close to the benefit of freeze dried food.

Store-bought freeze-dried food is expensive and full of junk fillers, chemicals and stuff I can't pronounce. When you freeze dry at home, you know the source of your food, who made it and when it was made. You can also bulk up on discount foods, fire sale items, foods that are at the end of their grocery store shelf life and so on. If you are savvy, you can spend very little money and get a whole bunch of quality freeze dried food. I am frugal as all get out, especially when it comes to food, but I am also a little picky when it comes to what I am putting into my body. Freeze drying is perfect for that. I have found that many grocery stores don't always sell a high quantity of the items that I like to eat (organic and specialty foods). This works in my favor big time. If they don't have enough people to buy these foods and they are closing them out or at the end of shelf life, they just want to break even or recoup some of their money. I will gladly take it off their hands, many times for ⅓ of what they originally had it priced at. We will talk about this later.

Going along with that last point, you can also freeze dry what type of food you want. The biggest negative, other than price and food quality, of commercially freeze dried food is that you are limited to the food selection in their lineup. That's fine if you want to eat the same 20 things, but most people would get tired of eating the same boring foods. With the 1000's of cycles I have run and the advice and experience of our freeze drying community, we are able to freeze dry just about anything at this point. With modifications of recipes or a small work around to modify recipes, all your favorite recipes can now be freeze dried. Check out our cookbook to see the most comprehensive recipes for freeze drying! www.freezedryingcookbook.com It's updated daily with new recipes, techniques, information and practices.

On this same point, people with specialty diets or health issues can also benefit from having an easy meal that can be quickly rehydrated with warm water. Whether you are on a business trip, road trip, family gathering, etc. where there are limited options, you can still eat what you want or need. Freeze dried food can easily stow in a backpack or purse and that makes it simple for your dietary needs to be satisfied.

NO FOOD GOES TO WASTE! That is not possible with any other type of food storage. Canning, freezing, dehydrating or dry storage all have their limitations, and when compared to freeze drying, do not compare. You can save every ounce of leftovers, take home the extra food from parties or gatherings, keep your thanksgiving turkey and all the stuffing safe until you are ready for them in the future. Even your wedding cake! Again, I am a frugal guy, and so is my wife. I absolutely hate throwing away food! We keep a few extra sets of FD trays (see "what you need for your freeze dryer" section) with extra sets of tray lids from www.freezedryingsupplies.com and any time there is food leftover or extra servings, it goes onto a tray with a lid and into the deep freeze. I just keep adding to the tray(s) until I have enough to do an entire leftover batch. I have leftovers that we freeze dried back in 2017 and that feels amazing. Each year Americans waste 119 billion pounds of food! It is estimated that over 40% of food goes to waste. That is both sad and extremely inefficient and wasteful. Think about what would happen if even 10% of Americans owned freeze dryers.

Gardening is another huge benefit for me. I find gardening therapeutic (and sometimes anti therapeutic :) and freeze drying goes hand in hand with gardening. A gardening magazine is where I was first introduced to freeze drying. But the biggest issue with gardening is going from no food in your garden, to having an abundance of one type of food. There are only a few ways to utilize all of that delicious pay off. You can try to eat it all before it goes bad, you can give some away or you can preserve it. If you try to eat all of it, you will either must get really creative with recipes or you will get so sick of that type of food, you may never want to eat it again. In order to preserve it, you can dehydrate it, can it or freeze dry it. If you choose to dehydrate or water bath can, you will not end up with the same product as you started with in most cases. Not all freeze dried food will turn out perfect when rehydrated either, but the options for what will preserve are far greater than the other options. Oh yeah, it will last lots longer too.

With that said, I like to visualize my freeze dried food as good as money in the bank. My food reserve bank. A currency, if you will. This is something that many people don't think about. The cost of food is not going down....ever. In 2022 alone, the cost of certain foods went up by 30%+. That's a scary situation for the future. Think about what the price of chicken was in 2001 in comparison to current prices. If I compared the return on investment for my chicken in 2017 to my other investments, it's probably the best ROI of any asset. Maybe more people need to start a Freeze Dried Food Portfolio! (Just kidding......sort of)

As I touched on earlier, if you are savvy, you can really get some great deals on food at the grocery store. Most larger grocery stores have a discount area, tucked away in the back or sometimes in a corner, with food that is getting close to expiration, slow moving or close out. Also, check the ads for sales. The cashiers will look at you funny when you bring 30 pounds of grapes to checkout, but the jokes on them! You are locking in the current price for pennies on the dollar if you crack those open in the future.

Another huge benefit of freeze drying is the 97% retention of nutrition in food. Dehydrating is often compared to freeze drying, but let's be honest, there is absolutely nothing comparable between the two. Sure, they are both removing water, but freeze drying removes 100% of the water and you are left with almost the full nutritional value, a shelf stable product for decades and the texture of the food remains the same or very similar. Try rehydrating some dehydrated food…. go ahead, try it!

I have found that freeze dried food is awesome for traveling. Whether you are piling into a car to drive across the country, RVing, or hopping on a plane, freeze dried food solves one huge problem. The lack of refrigeration. All you need is a little water or depending on what you are eating, maybe no water. As I mentioned earlier, I am somewhat choosy when it comes to my diet, and we travel quite a bit. When you are on the open road, the choices of food are underwhelming to say the least. I love a greasy cheeseburger as much as the next guy, but one is plenty. If you are traveling for hours or even days, we dip into our freeze dried food bank and have meals of easy and healthy food. The best part is, we don't have to bring a big cooler to pack food into. There is a real sense of satisfaction when you can go to your food storage and pull out 3, 4 or more days' worth of meals that are lightweight, compact and easy to make. I used to have a deep freeze (or two) full of frozen food. Now I don't even own a deep freeze. All my food storage or extra food is either freeze dried or in my refrigerator's freezer. That may not suit everyone's needs, but it works for me. I do recommend keeping at least enough room in your refrigerator freezer to freeze your freeze dryer trays. If you are traveling by plane, from my experience, TSA won't give you grief about it either. Mainly because most of the public doesn't even know what freeze dried food is.

Why do I need to freeze dry?

Freeze drying is not for the unmotivated. You must have a good reason to put in all the work to cook, prepare and store all this food. Many folks are preppers who want a sustainable food source, during tragic times, financial crisis, natural disasters etc. You might ask 10 freeze dryers why they freeze dry and you might get 10 different answers. I can't give you your reason to freeze dry, but I suspect if you are getting ready to slap down several thousand dollars and you are reading this book, you probably already know why.

Here are a few other reasons:

*Food prices (they only go up; FD food is like having money in a high yield savings account)

*Natural disasters (the perfect food when there is no power)

*Camping & hunting (my favorite use for freeze dried food)

*Backpacking & hiking (it's lightweight and quick to make)

*Prepping (the ultimate food storage item)

*Alternative uses include taxidermy, document recovery, electronics recovery, soil, seeds, flowers and herbs

*Picnics

*Meals for soldiers overseas

*Meals for the elderly or diet specific

*Christmas or holiday gifts

*Food storage

*Travel

*Selling freeze dried food as a business

*Specialty diets

*Easy premade lunches for work

*Road trips

Another thing that will help you understand freeze drying is to understand how the freeze dryer works and what it does. Check out the next chapter to see how.

Chapter 2

How does the freeze dryer work?

Another thing that will help you understand freeze drying is to understand how the freeze dryer works and what it does. One of the coolest things about freeze drying (at least for me) is it feels like a grown-up science experiment. I have a new way of looking at not only foods, but soil, electronics etc. and asking myself "will this freeze dry?" or "I wonder what would happen if" …..But how does the freeze dryer work? How can it take 100% of water out of food? Without some kind of NASA technology. Well, it does use NASA technology. Freeze drying was originally designed in WWII to preserve medication for wounded soldiers. In the 1960's NASA revisited the technology because they needed a way for astronauts to have an easy to make meal with little prep and no refrigeration. If you really think about it that's what most freeze dryers want as well. I'm no astronaut or a NASA engineer, but I will do my best to explain how the freeze dryer does what it does. Freeze drying is also called lyophilization. It sounds complicated but it basically means an item is frozen, then put under extreme vacuum and then heated. This turns the water content (which is now frozen and in a solid form) into a vapor which then sticks to the side of the vacuum chamber in the form of ice. The vacuum in the chamber is what pulls the vapor to the side of the chamber. The Harvestright freeze dryer is very similar to a commercial unit, but in a smaller form. You have a refrigeration unit that will bring the food down to below zero temperatures (sometimes -40). It also has a vacuum pump that is external from the machine that creates the vacuum needed. The vacuum chamber is a stainless-steel barrel shaped chamber in the center of the machine that houses a rack. Depending on what size freeze dryer you purchase, it may have 3, 4, 5 up to 8 shelves on the rack. The tops of each shelf have a rubber-like heating pad that turns on and off through the freeze drying cycle to slowly heat up the frozen food under vacuum. The entire freeze dryer is communicating to sensors and software and when the machine recognizes that there is little to no resistance left, the food is free from moisture. The freeze drying software assumes at this point that your freeze dried food is complete.

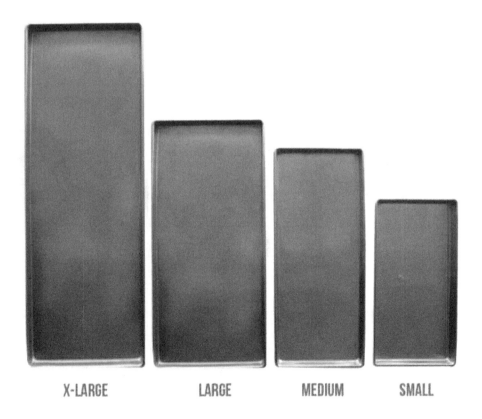

X-LARGE   LARGE   MEDIUM   SMALL

<u>What size freeze dryer should I get?</u>

This info is specifically for the Harvestright freeze dryer. **As time goes on, I'm sure there** will be other brands available, but this may still be relevant and should give you something to consider. There are several factors that you need to take into consideration before, and hopefully not AFTER you purchase a freeze dryer. First, you need to determine how much food you want to freeze dry. The info below gives how much each tray holds and how much each cycle will yield. Keep in mind that **it's** not very practical or efficient to run half loads.

Small Freeze Dryer

Each tray holds 5 cups

3 trays = 15 Cup total capacity

4-7 lbs per batch

Medium Freeze Dryer

Each tray holds 6 cups

4 trays = 24 Cup total capacity

7-10 lbs per batch

Large Freeze Dryer

Each tray holds 8 cups

5 trays = 40 Cup total capacity

12-16 lbs per batch

XL Freeze Dryer 6 trays

Each tray holds 11-12 cups

6 trays = 66-72 cup total capacity

30-35 lbs. per batch

*These are suggested capacities as a helpful tool and not a representation of manufacturers recommendations.

Other things to consider before purchasing.

When determining what size freeze dryer to get there are a few more factors you need to consider. Most people naturally gravitate to the large or XL because bigger is always better, right? I was in the same boat. I have owned a large freeze dryer and loved it, but after several years of freeze drying, I got to a point where it was almost too much! Wait, TOO MUCH freeze dried food? It's a great problem to have but a large does as much food as a small and a medium put together. That adds up very quickly and I got to a point where I was almost forcing myself to fill up trays. The large and XL are an excellent way to stock up your food supply fast, but for some, it may not be practical for the long term.

You'll also want to make sure you have enough room and space for the size you want to purchase. The freeze dryer footprint is like a dorm fridge, beverage cooler or dishwasher and although they have gotten smaller through the years, it still takes up a good amount of space in your home. You can go to harvestright's website to see general specs of the current models. The space, along with the noise that it produces are something to consider. You may have a spot picked out that gives you plenty of space for your freeze drying activities, but if it's next to your bedroom and the walls are paper thin, you may want to reconsider.

Another deciding factor is also your electrical situation. The large and XL freeze dryer requires a dedicated 20-amp circuit for them to operate correctly and safely. If you don't have a dedicated circuit to run this on, you will either need to have an electrician run a circuit just for your freeze dryer or you may want to look into a medium or small that can just run on any ol' 110 style outlet. If you go with a dedicated circuit, you also need to know that it requires a NEMA style plug/ outlet. Not a big deal, but it will not work without it. The other thing to think about is once you put in a circuit specifically for the freeze dryer, you cannot move it away from that location. DO NOT use extension cords! It will void your warranty and is also a great way to start an electrical fire.

A big factor that not everyone takes into consideration is the noise that a freeze dryer makes. This pertains to all sizes of freeze dryers. The freeze dryer has many similar components as a refrigerator or freezer. If you know how loud your fridge is, it's a little louder than that. It's a lot of fan type noise similar to an air conditioning unit. I realize that is a huge spectrum of noise level, so before you buy, try to hear one for yourself. On top of that, you have a vacuum pump running through most of the cycle. At the time this is being written there are two vacuum pump options. Consider yourself lucky because just a year ago, there were 4! The oiled pump is relatively quiet and I would compare the noise to a dishwasher. There is also an oil less pump that is considered maintenance free. Both are a suitable option for the freeze dryer, but when it comes to where the freeze dryer goes, it might drive you nuts if you don't have a place to get away from it. If you live in an apartment or townhome, you may want to check out some of my videos on decibel levels. I'm not saying you can't do it, but if your walls are thin, you may end up with grumpy neighbors or you might not be able to sleep while it's running.

While we are on the topic of location, let's dive into a few more variables that you need to consider. Going back to the size of the freeze dryer you want to purchase, make sure you have enough space for your freeze drying and food bagging or processing. The location you choose for your freeze drying area also needs to be climate controlled and the ideal temperature kept around 60-70 degrees. If it's too hot, your cycles will become much longer, and you are adding lots of extra stress to the machine. Heat and humidity counteract the freeze drying process. If you live in a humid area, sometimes it can be hard to get away from. Since I started freeze drying, I have lived in the Rocky Mountains and the plains of the midwest and back again. I can safely say that my freeze dryer works much better in the dry air of the Rockies than it does in the humid damp climate of the midwest. Why? because the humidity is counterproductive. Freeze drying is removing moisture from the food and when you are in a very humid area, the machine has to work much harder to accomplish that. You can also consider adding a dehumidifier to your freeze drying area. A well-ventilated area never hurts either. The freeze dryer puts out a good amount of heat and if you can move that heat away from the freeze dryer, you are saving some wear and tear and some cycle time on the machine. I have seen some people put in crazy ventilation systems just to circulate air around their freeze-drying area. Now that's dedication, but a simple box fan can usually move enough air to make a difference if needed.

The freeze dryer also takes some maintenance to keep it up to snuff and ensure you have an appliance that lasts a long time. The freeze dryer itself should be routinely cleaned. The interior should be cleaned to keep it free from bacteria and mildew. The exterior should be cleaned to keep the dust and debris out of the refrigeration unit area. The machine is very similar to a refrigerator or freezer and keeping those "dust bunnies" out of the inside of your freeze dryer will help it run cooler and more efficiently. The refrigeration system is also Freon based like a refrigerator freezer and at some point, will need some attention. There is not much data out there on this which is hopefully a good sign that the units will last a very long time.

The freeze dryer vacuum pump is the heart and soul of the freeze dryer and because it's the workhorse, it also means that this is the part of the freeze dryer that is most prone to failure. If you are going to ignore maintenance on any part of the FD, make sure it's not the pump. Whether you choose to purchase the oiled vacuum pump or the oil less vacuum pump, both require maintenance at some point. The next section will cover this in depth.

Chapter 3

Which Pump Should I Buy?

Many people struggle with which pump they should purchase. Currently, there are only 2 choices, and both are good options. Consider yourself lucky, the first vacuum pump that I owned needed to have an oil change EVERY load! I will refer to the past options later in this section in case you have an older model or are considering buying a used unit. As of this writing you can either go for the Premier Oiled Pump (lime green) or the Oil less pump. They are both great options but require some degree of maintenance or rebuild at certain intervals. The oiled vacuum pump requires infrequent oil changes but the oil less (which used to be called the maintenance free pump) requires a rebuild every 2,000-3,000 hours of use. So, you can either put in the maintenance with oil changes or send in your oil less every year or two to have Harvestright rebuild it on your dime. Here is a head-to-head comparison based on my experience on owning all of them. Keep in mind that pumps will change over time and these writings may not apply. I also have several videos on this topic that you can reference.

Premier Pump

If you watch my videos, it is no secret that I am pretty set on this pump as being my favorite. So much in fact, that I own 2 of them. Yes, it does require oil changes, but only every 25-30 cycles. For me and most **average freeze dryers, that's once every couple of months. Even if you are running your freeze dryer nonstop, you will only be changing the oil once per month. The oil changes are quick and simple and can be done in a matter of minutes. It also uses less than a quart of vacuum pump oil. It's also more efficient, it's quiet, smooth and in my opinion will last a long time for a few reasons. First, it's lubricated with oil. That means if you treat it well, it will treat you well. The only bad thing I have found with the premier pump is the "fog" that you may have heard about. That "fog" is water vapor being released from the oil chamber. That means there is 0 to very little water that can corrode parts inside of the vacuum pump because it expels it into the air. This sometimes creates a "fog" during freeze drying. I like to put on a wig and treat this as my 80's rock metal practice. When life gives you lemons.......

The oil less does shed water as well, but in my opinion, not as well. It needs to be run for several minutes after each use to flush the water from the components. I could have changed my oil in that time, but I only must do that every 25-30 cycles. Don't get me wrong, I am not saying the oil less is not a great pump. For many people, they simply do not want to mess with changing oil or have oil around their finished food products. This makes it a good choice for commercial or business type settings. Also, if you do not have to change oil at certain intervals, you never really have to think about it until it needs a rebuild. It also does produce more heat and bigger noise readings, so please keep this in mind when deciding.

Oilless Pump

The oil less does shed water as well, but in my opinion, not as well. It needs to be run for several minutes after each use to flush the water from the components. I could have changed my oil in that time, but I only have to do that every 25-30 cycles. Don't get me wrong, I am not saying the oil less is not a great pump. For many people, they simply do not want to mess with changing oil or have oil around their finished food products. This makes it a good choice for commercial or business type settings. Also, if you do not have to change oil at certain intervals, you never really have to think about it until it needs a rebuild. The oil less pump can be a great option for those of you that want to press it and forget it freeze drying. It does require some maintenance at specific intervals as mentioned earlier but for some that can be worth it. Rebuilds aside, this pump is built like a tank! It's very good quality and similar vacuum pumps in the scientific freeze drying industry go for much more than you pay for these from Harvestright. Good quality does however mean it weighs a lot! The noise level of this pump is more substantial than the premier which can be a factor when considering where it will be placed. It also puts off quite a bit of heat as it does not have oil to keep it running cool. It is air cooled, so keep this in mind when considering this pump.

A History of Freeze Dryer Pumps

Here is a quick history of past and present vacuum pump options. Use this for future knowledge or if you are considering buying a pre-owned freeze dryer. If you are purchasing pre-owned and the vacuum pump is a JB Eliminator, I would suggest upgrading to at least the standard model to save yourself some grief.

JB Eliminator- This model was the first version sold until around 2018 I believe. It was a workhorse and got a whole lot of freeze dryers, a whole bunch of freeze dried food. However, it had a slew of problems and quirks. First off, this was a vacuum pump that was designed for the HVAC industry among other things, but not designed to shed the water that gets into freeze dryer oil. The internals were steel and not stainless or a non-rusting metal, so it created lots of issues when it started to corrode inside the oil chamber. I remember my first time removing the cover to clean the inside of the chamber and thinking "this thing is toast." The models that were available after the JB Eliminator each got better and better at shedding that water from the oil in various ways. The current pumps now are specifically designed with freeze drying in mind and are on a whole different level than the JB. It also had to have its oil changed every cycle. You read that right, EVERY SINGLE CYCLE. I won't sugar coat it. It sucked. It was also loud, ran extremely hot and was very heavy. Freeze drying pumps have come a long way since 2017.

<u>Standard Pump-</u> Sometime around 2017 Harvestright decided it was time to bid farewell to the JB Eliminator. It was preceded by the Standard pump which now only needed to have its oil changed every 5 cycles. Freeze dryers rejoiced as this was the pump that came

with every freeze dryer until there was an oil less option upgrade. There were a few versions of this pump as far as I can tell but these were much quieter and smoother and a much-welcomed improvement.

<u>Oilless "Eagle" Pump-</u>

A much-needed option after having to change oil every cycle in the JB Eliminator. It was and still is a suitable freeze drying pump but shares all of the same characteristics as the current

version mentioned above but worse at most of the negative points mentioned earlier. There have been several improvements over the years and some cosmetic differences as well.

Oilless Scroll Pump-

This was a short-lived model that was quieter, smaller, and less expensive than the "eagle". I owned one for a brief time because I _wanted_ to test all the available pump options at that time. It was quieter, had a smaller footprint and seemed pretty maintenance free other than the recommended dry flush after each cycle. I noticed after a month or so of use, that it was not shedding water as well as the other options and it felt like a lesser quality pump that also seemed to pull a weaker vacuum than the others. It worked just fine for the  time I owned it, but I questioned its longevity. Many people still own and use theirs daily, but I am happy to see that Harvestright is constantly trying to improve the freeze drying experience and decided to give current users better options.

Premier Pump- As far as I know there have been two generations of this premier pump. The one pictured here is the first generation and the one pictured earlier is the second generation. They are meant to look the same, but the first generation seems to be a little better quality. For good reason because the first generation used to be an expensive upgrade. It does **seem to be built a little better and it's a bigger pump.** Other than that, I don't know the exact specifics. The second generation was included with the purchase of a freeze dryer (no longer an upgrade) after the standard pump was phased out around 2021. I own both generations (one for a backup). Side by side they appear similar. I love these pumps because they are efficient, smooth, quiet and dependable. They require very little maintenance and from my experience, they are very dependable. I'll put it this way: I do freeze drying as a job and this is the pump I choose even though it's not the most expensive option. If there were a better choice, I would use it.

XL Premier Pump-

This is the most recent release of vacuum pumps. It became available with the XL freeze dryer and is suited for the larger chamber and capacity of the XL. I have little to no experience with this pump at the time of this writing. I have only owned this pump for a few weeks but if it's anything like its smaller version, it will give many years of use.

Chapter 4

I Just Bought a freeze dryer…. Now What?

If you are going to be a freeze dryer, you need to be prepared. Chances are if you are buying a freeze dryer, you are already the type of person who is prepared anyhow. There are several things that you will want to consider purchasing prior or have ready for when your freeze dryer shows up. This way, you are ready to freeze dry instead of spending hours getting your space ready. You also need to prepare yourself for delivery. We will cover both in this section.

The Delivery of Your Freeze Dryer

The freeze dryer is big no matter what size you order and will come freight from FedEx or another freight carrier depending on where you live. A few things you should know before you crack into that box. Even though you are excited to get going, ALWAYS, ALWAYS inspect the box before you sign anything or let the delivery person leave. I have heard way too many stories about people accepting damaged boxes and then they are on the hook for all damages, mishandling or even worse, missing items. Once that delivery person leaves, the delivery company is no longer liable for anything. They might not want very badly to wait for you to inspect, but it could cost you dearly. The freeze dryers are usually only banded a couple of times, so take some scissors, cut those bands and inspect the goods. Then just when you thought you were ready to start freeze drying! Nope. You need to let that machine sit level for at least 24 hours. If it was moved around or tipped to the side, upside down or inside and out, all the components need to settle. Many of the components of a freeze dryer are just like a refrigerator or freezer. While you are waiting, you can go through the next section and begin to set up your machine. There are also some things you can check out and do to prepare as well. Go through the *"What's in the Box?"* and the *"Setting up your freeze dryer"* section while you are waiting. That info can be found later in the book.

First, you need to prepare yourself for the delivery. It will come on a skid or pallet, so you need to make sure you have a place for a large truck to deliver or a predetermined area to meet the driver. My recommendation, if possible, is to get the delivery as close to the spot you are going to leave it permanently. Freeze dryers are heavy and you will need at least two people to move it into place. Do yourself a favor and have your freeze drying space ready so you can set this thing in its new home and get freeze drying. One other thing that you need to know! The freeze dryer needs to rest in its place for about 24-36 hours before you put your first freeze drying load in. The internals are much like an air conditioning unit or refrigerator and it's best to let oils, fluids etc. settle into their place before using. If you don't you may have problems from the start. My suspicion is that a good portion of the people that have problems when first getting their freeze dryer either didn't install something properly, didn't read the manual and/or they did not let their freeze dryer and pump rest for the recommended time. These are complex appliances that need your full attention until you have a grasp on them. Commit to being educated and confident on how they work and how to keep them in optimal condition. They are not for the faint of heart and are certainly not turn-key (although they are getting closer with every new version). They do require minor adjustments and problem solving at times.

Setting Up Your Workspace

Placement of your freeze dryer is a tough decision, but figuring out where you are going to put your freeze dryer is a very important decision. You will need to factor in several things before choosing your "spot". You will need a space that accounts for noise, heat and cold, well ventilated, and preferably has room to prep and package as well. The noise can be a pivotal factor and I would not recommend putting it in your kitchen, living room or your bedroom. The machine runs for 24-48 hours on average and although it's not extremely loud, after that amount of time, a constant humming or buzzing will drive you crazy or lose sleep. Maybe that's just me. Usually, a spare bedroom or the basement is sufficient for most users and gives enough space from living areas that it's not a nuisance. If you have the luxury of choosing a space, always choose the larger area. You will find out quickly that the more comfortable your work area is, the more you're willing to freeze dry and ultimately you will find more enjoyment in the whole process.

Something else that needs to be addressed is the amount of heat that a freeze dryer puts out. If your space is confined and you cannot ventilate or move a significant amount of air around with a fan, you may want to think twice about that space. If you live in a warm area, you can possibly put it in your garage as well. If it's not too humid or the garage is climate controlled, that can potentially be the best spot in the house. Your work area needs to be well ventilated and climate controlled. If not, it can put unnecessary stress on the freeze dryer and be completely counterproductive as mentioned earlier.

From my experience, the key to the perfect space is all of the above but also not being too far away from your kitchen or prep area. If the machine is too far away or in a spot that you don't go into often, it's easy to forget to use it. For some it may be a nuisance to go up and down stairs to check on the freeze dryer during the cycle. Put it far enough away that it's not annoying, but close enough that you can easily check on it and you are encouraged to use it. You can also consider getting a wi-fi camera to always have eyes on the freeze dryer. We will cover that and other tips in the next section.

Things to buy before your freeze dryer arrives.

Here are some things to consider buying. I will include my preferred items with a link and a picture when I can. If you type the link directly into your browser bar, you can get directly to my preferred products. I know this can be a pain, but if you are reading this as a hardcopy book, this is unfortunately the best way. If you want to just skip each individual link, you can just go to my Amazon store link http://www.amazon.com/shop/retiredat40 and find the majority of the items listed below and make sure you go to www.freezedryingsupplies.com to see all of the accessories listed below. Not all of these may be necessary to suit your needs, but this should give you a great start on setting up your space and help with food preparation. It may also spawn some alternative ideas for your situation.

Rolling Cart- https://amzn.to/3kMy8Ti   If your workspace is tight or you just like being able to move things around, a cart is very handy for keeping the freeze dryer elevated and mobile. I also like having mine on a cart because I can keep my pump, drain bucket and extra supplies on the bottom shelf. This one will hold up to 500 lbs and gives you enough room to have your pump next to it or a small prep area to the side. Verify this will fit your freeze dryer size, or make sure you can modify it slightly if needed. The measurements of freeze dryers change from time to time, so check the latest specs.

Stainless Worktable- https://amzn.to/3ZjH5IH These stainless worktables are very handy for many different purposes. I like them because they are sturdy and don't stain. They come in many different sizes and not only can you use them to prep and package your food, but you can also use them to set your freeze dryer on. They are rated for several hundred pounds. They will also hold the XL freeze dryer.

Dedicated Outlet- https://amzn.to/3WBTEXR for the large and XLfreeze dryers, a dedicated 20-amp outlet with a NEMA 5-20 style plug is required. If you do not have this capability or type available, I would have one installed (professionally) or reconsider purchasing a small or medium. If you are purchasing a medium, a 20 amp is not required by the manufacturer, but I would highly suggest it. If you have a newer home with arc fault breakers, you may have some issues if you don't have a dedicated 20 amp as well (even with the medium). The medium is designed to run on a 15-amp 120V outlet that can be found in any home, but I have seen mine occasionally go over 15 amps and trip a breaker. If your freeze dryer trips a breaker and you don't realize it within a few hours, your cycle may be compromised. Also, make sure that you are not using power strips or extension cords as they can void your warranty and jeopardize your safety.

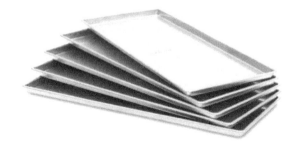

Extra trays- This is one of the most essential "extras" you can get. Having an extra set or several extra sets of trays means you can store leftovers or prep your next batch of food while the freeze dryer is running with the first set. As of this writing, Harvestright is the only place that produces trays for their freeze

dryers. For nice quality, thick stainless steel trays, I find them to be reasonably priced. You can find

them at: **https://affiliates.harvestright.com/416.html**

Killowatt Meter- https://amzn.to/3kHJkjX One of the biggest
concerns that people have before purchasing a freeze dryer is the
amount of electricity a freeze dryer uses. The quick answer is
between $1-3 per load. With a power consumption meter like this,
you can keep track of the kilowatt hours used. This can be helpful
for deciding what time of day you are going to run your freeze dryer
as well as determining if you want to freeze dry certain types of

foods. Also, once you have a log of power usage, you can convert your kilowatt hours to a cost per

month, year or batch.

Oil Filter- https://amzn.to/3Jad1V0 Unless you are purchasing a

used freeze dryer, chances are your new freeze dryer came with an

oil filter. Harvestright started including their own branded oil filter

around 2020 and it works great and is tailored to freeze drying needs.

If you don't have one of their oil filters, you can buy a Brita style

pitcher like this one and hollow out the filter area. Once you have

hollowed that out. Stuff some toilet paper, coffee filter or similar

material in there to run your oil through. This will separate the

particles and some moisture from the oil allowing you to reuse the vacuum pump oil over and over.

For more details, I have a video on how to make a DIY oil filter. Follow this link:

https://youtu.be/KuqEJNcuJql

Clip mount fan- https://amzn.to/3XUCxld The freeze dryer and

vacuum pump can put out a lot of heat. Having a small fan

running to circulate air can drastically cool the environment around

the freeze dryer. This one is the one I use because it can be run

wireless/ rechargeable or wired and it has a clip that can attach to

parts and pieces so it can be strategically placed. Another great

use for the fan is in the defrost cycle of the freeze dryer. A small

fan helps the heating pads melt the built-up ice after the cycle is

done. We will talk more in depth to this later in the book.

Food Scale- https://amzn.to/3HwCarB Weighing food before and

after freeze drying is extremely important for getting a proper

rehydration formula. An accurate kitchen scale that is movable and

has a large-scale area is helpful for this. I have found that weighing

in grams is the easiest way to determine how much water needs to

be added back into the food to rehydrate to the amount it was before

freeze drying. I like this model because it has a large-scale area, it can run off batteries or plugged in

and the display can also be wall mounted.

Bamboo steamer basket- https://amzn.to/3R9V2QE

A bamboo steamer is an inexpensive way to slowly rehydrate difficult

and stubborn freeze dried foods. It rehydrates with a gentle steam.

We will cover this and other alternative ways to rehydrate later in the

book.

Instant Pot- https://amzn.to/3Jeq9Z4 An instant pot or a slow cooker

is such a versatile way to cook in large batches for freeze drying. I also

love it for easy, hands-off meals, but another thing an instant pot does

well is rehydration. If you use the rack that sits at the bottom of the

instant pot (most come with this), you can put a small amount of water

at the bottom of the instant pot, and it will keep your food elevated

above the water all while steaming it under pressure. This is great for dense or difficult freeze dried

foods.

Mason Jars- https://amzn.to/3R3V0tr For freeze dried food, you only have a few storage options: 5-7 mil Mylar food storage bags, #10 cans or mason jars. For short term or almost immediate use,

mason jars are an excellent option for storage. They are airtight and can be sealed over and over. If sealed properly, these can be a great option for 1-3 year storage. We will cover the limitations of mason jars in our food storage section later in the book. Check out the next item to see how you can seal these without air.

Avid Armor Vacuum Chamber Sealer- Other than the freeze dryer, this is my favorite toy for freeze drying! It has so many uses! It has a marinate function that opens pores of meats and foods to inject them with flavor before cooking or freeze drying. This is also extremely helpful when rehydrating. When you rehydrate under a vacuum, it not only speeds the process, but also helps inject flavors into the dry pores

of freeze dried food. You can take your freeze dried food to a whole different flavor level when you get creative with injecting flavors into the food. Imagine rehydrating your beef, chicken or pork with a marinade that goes straight into the pores of the meat. When the freeze dried food is rehydrated under vacuum, it hydrates much faster and more efficiently. You can also use this to pull out 99%+ of the air inside a food storage bag or mason jar with the available attachment. It adds an extra layer of protection for your freeze dried food in Mylar food storage bags. I do still recommend using an oxygen absorber when using this because the chamber vacuum sealer cannot always get all air and oxygen out. Adding the oxygen absorber can remove trace amounts that are leftover. When you vacuum seal, it also compacts the bag size for easier storage and if you package it properly, allows you to lay most foods flat. This takes up lots less room in storage and allows you to organize more effectively. If you are thinking about ordering one of these, I can get you 10% off through this link! https://avidarmor.com?aff=43 Enter the promo code LIVELIFESIMPLE at checkout.

Mason Jar Sealer attachment- https://amzn.to/3Jjm99N

This is used to remove air from mason jars and seal them at the same time. It can be used with many styles of food saver devices if it has a hose accessory port. If you use this in conjunction with an oxygen absorber, you can drastically extend the shelf life of freeze dried food in mason jars. See additional tips on how to extend the shelf life in the *food storage* section found later in the book.

Food Processor- https://amzn.to/3XFjQSX A good quality food processor is vital for powdering and processing freeze dried foods. Why? Some foods like milk, eggs, dairy, juices, herbs etc. will not only rehydrate better when in powder form, but they will store better as well. I use powdered yogurt, kale, ginger, lemon etc. almost daily for my morning smoothie and for cooking. Powdered foods are often nutrient dense, more flavorful and can often be made from things that would normally go to waste (lemon and orange skins, vegetable waste can be turned into bullion).

<u>Vacuum sealable containers-</u> https://amzn.to/3ZVHdsO

If you have foods that are used frequently (freeze dried garlic, vegetable broth) or just want snacks that are easily accessible (freeze dried strawberries), then you should consider a resealable vacuum container. This container is great to set out on the counter or in your freeze dried pantry and it can be quickly resealed using the vacuum sealer. Use it over and over and keep your freeze dried food fresh.

<u>Sous Vide Cooker-</u> https://amzn.to/3XUEv4U Big things come in small packages. This is quickly becoming one of my favorite kitchen tools for freeze drying! It is only about the size of a big flashlight, but it cooks food perfectly every time and can be amazing for rehydration. The most tender foods and freeze dried foods were a result of the sous vide. A sous vide works like this. You put the food you would like to cook into a food saver style bag and seal it. I often use vegetables, garnishes, broths and spices in the bag as well. Fill the bag with broth, juice or water until the item is submerged. Seal the bag and

place in a large pot that the sous vide attaches to. The sous vide heats the water to the desired temperature and holds it there the duration of the cook time. The cook time can be entered manually or by using the app with built in recipes. The food cooks in its own juices and renders a tender, flavorful finished product that is unmatched. For freeze dried food, this is particularly beneficial, because when you introduce freeze dried food to a liquid, it absorbs it quickly. You can imagine all the creative ways you can now inject huge flavor into what you are cooking.

Thermal camera- https://amzn.to/3Y2u7ln A
thermal camera is a helpful tool when trying to
determine if your freeze dried food is completely
done. It does not detect moisture, but it does detect
the coldest spot of the tray which can help you
determine whether the food still has cold spots. You
can set the camera to give the coldest and warmest

spots in the camera frame and also set it to show freezing temps in the color blue. If it shows blue on

the trays or you have a spot that 30-40 degrees or lower, your food would not be complete because

there are still cold or frozen areas. If you understand how freeze drying works, then you know that

your food and trays need to be warm when done. The thermal camera I use attaches to your phone

and uses the phone's screen and computer. This makes it much less expensive than other options

but still gives it lots of features. This tool is not a necessity for freeze dryers but is very helpful

especially with thick or dense foods.

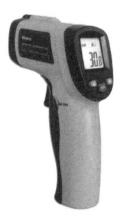

Infrared Thermometer- https://amzn.to/3wxZnmV This is a less
expensive way of determining cold spots in your food similar to the
thermal camera, just not as accurate. You can pinpoint specific
spots that you are concerned about and it will give you a
temperature reading back. It's a bit more time consuming and not
quite as effective as the thermal camera but is still helpful in
locating cold spots.

Vibration absorption- https://amzn.to/3j3odlv Vibration can cause a lot
of extra racket when you are running your freeze dryer. Your main freeze
drying unit and the vacuum pump put out a fair amount of vibration. If

you can dampen that vibration from resonating through other things, like the table or cart that the freeze dryer sits on, you can reduce the noise the freeze dryer makes. These inexpensive pads or something similar can be placed under the feet or better yet under the entire pump or freeze dryer to help.

Vacuum Pump oil- If you have an oiled pump, it's highly recommended that you have at least one additional quart of approved vacuum pump oil. At some point, you will need an additional quart and if you don't have it on hand, it could hold up your next freeze drying batch. I have always used Robinair premium vacuum pump oil and I am very happy with it. There are many other choices that are great quality as well such as Navak,

Black Gold etc. but please verify that your choice is an adequate and approved oil from Harvestright or your vacuum pump manufacturer.

Bottle brush- https://amzn.to/3Jiy2N7 The first time you make a mess inside your freeze drying chamber and your tray rack, you will thank me for turning you on to this brush. This brush fits perfectly in between the shelves on the tray rack and can scrub all those tough to get places. It's also long enough to get from front to back and it scrubs both top and bottom at the same time.

<u>Reolink or Wifi camera-</u> https://amzn.to/3XHylp6 I hope someday, somebody will be reading this and this product will no longer be needed. One of the most annoying things about freeze drying is the inability to determine when a load will be finished. You can get a decent guess of how long the load will take and start it at a certain time of the day accordingly, but you will, at some point, finish a load at 2 am or when you are running errands, or at work. At least if you have a wi-fi camera set up, you can glance at your phone to see where the cycle is at and how much sleep you can anticipate. This model is extra great because you can set a motion detector on it that will alert you when something moves on the screen (ie. when **your screen changes from drying to "process complete") and it** also has night vision. I hope that at some point freeze dryers will just have an integrated app that will give all of this information. Changing things from your phone (like additional time) would be amazing!

<u>Deep freeze-</u> https://amzn.to/404JWjK **If you don't** already have one and you want to get the most out of your freeze dryer, a deep freeze can get you there. Many people already own a deep freeze **and if you find a smokin' deal on sale** the freeze dryer allows you to preserve large amounts of food before they get freezer burned or go bad. This is yet another reason to pick up extra trays and some tray lids. You can portion out a sale item, freeze it in your deep freeze

and when the freeze dryer is open, toss it in there and 25-40 hours later have another addition to your long term storage. You can also make large batches of food and have trays frozen in the deep freeze.

Labeler/ labels- https://amzn.to/3Hdq3yb It's important to have clearly labeled bags and jars when you are storing large amounts of food. It might be easy to remember contents, dates, instructions etc. now, but 10 years down the road if you are not labeled and organized, you could have a serious

problem on your hands. Whether you buy a label maker like this one, or labels that stick onto a bag or you write on the food storage bag with a permanent marker, make sure you have your food clearly labeled. Your future self will thank you.

Supplies and Accessories for Your Freeze Dryer

When I started freeze drying, there weren't a lot of aftermarket freeze drying supplies out there, especially ones that helped with 3 of the biggest problems with freeze drying: Storage, organization & packaging the products. The products that freeze dryers needed were not available, so we built them ourselves. When we started www.freezedryingsupplies.com from the ground up in 2020 we had already been freeze drying for several years and had the knowledge of what freeze dryers wanted and how to streamline the biggest obstacles in freeze drying. We designed and manufactured all of our accessories locally and we are proud to say we are MADE IN THE USA. This is not always an easy feat, but this is something that is very important to us. We also developed the products to be FDA approved and able to withstand the extreme temperatures of freeze dryers. We are constantly at the drawing board coming up with new products, new solutions and improvements for freeze drying. Here are the items that we sell at www.freezedryingsupplies.com that will help solve the storage/ organization & packaging problems of freeze dryers.

Corner Tray Stackers- These are universal for Small, Medium or Large Trays (and will accommodate any size Freeze Dryer tray edges. These are new and improved stackers and the only available that "lock" onto your freeze dryer pan and prevent them from slipping off. Stack your trays with confidence. These hold the trays together tight and will not slip around like some others that are out there. Compatible with our other products including Tray Dividers, Silicone tray liners, pre-cut tray Parchment paper etc.

Use these tray stackers for pre-freezing your food to save money, space and have the freeze dryer ready for the next batch! These are food grade and dishwasher safe! Get multiple sets to stack as high as you have room for.

Made in USA

Tray dividers- These make your freeze dryer trays portion making machines. They are designed to fit Harvest Right trays and are fully adjustable to make many different portion sizes. Interlocking molds make adjustable grids that stay together with a knife edge on one side allowing you to cut through tough foods. Easy grip tabs, sturdy, durable, dishwasher safe and FDA approved, BPA free material. Made to withstand freeze drying temperatures. These are also compatible with our tray stackers, silicone sheets, pre-cut parchment, and tray lids.

Tray lids- The "Original" is the first (and best) freeze dryer tray lid. These are a great way to store leftovers or extra trays that are in the "cue" for the freeze dryer. Ours stack and hold neatly on top of each other which is great for the fridge or freezer. You can stack these as tall as your space will allow. Avoid spoiled or freezer burned food. They are also clear plastic for viewing contents of the tray. Snaps at all 4 corners and can also be used with our tray dividers.

Food Funnel- This is our new and improved Food Funnel. It's 18" wide and is plenty big to accommodate any size freeze dryer tray. This helps direct your freeze dried food into a storage bag or mason jar instead of all over the floor. You can purchase this with the adjustable stand or the funnel

by itself. The funnel stand is adjustable so you can set it to your desired height for filling different sized bags, jars and containers. The spout will also fit into a wide mouth or small mouth mason jar. This is a very sturdy funnel made from thick bpa free FDA approved plastic that makes packaging your freeze dried food a breeze!

Mylar Bags- we sell 8 x 12 Quart Size Mylar bags that are 5.5 mil thickness. (We're working on

larger sizes as well). These are MADE IN THE USA!! I dare you to find another company that can say that. These also have a gusseted bottom that holds the bag upright (great for use with the Food Funnel) and a zipper top that's resealable. One side has a label section for contents, rehydration and notes for easy organization.

Oxygen absorbers-

Our oxygen absorbers come as packages of 10 to reduce exposure, waste and resealing. These will absorb 180 - 300% of their rating. These also include oxygen indicators to ensure they are ready for use.

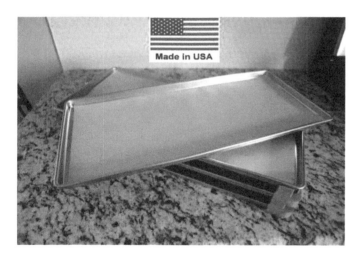

Pre-Cut Parchment Paper- No more fumbling. These parchment paper sheets are custom fit for your freeze dryer trays. Select which size tray size you need (comes in packs of 100 sheets). Can be reused if not damaged. You can also fold and dump contents into storage.

Silicone Mats/ tray liners- Color matched to our signature green color! Made of FDA Approved Material. Reusable, Durable and Easy to Clean with soap and water. Radius corners to fit perfectly in your FD pans. Available for small, medium, large and XL freeze dryers.

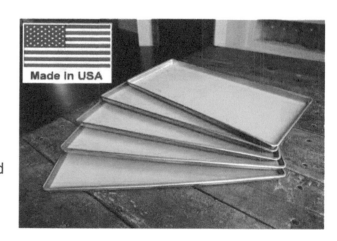

No suck / Anti-siphon kit- There is no worse feeling than a batch of freshly freeze dried food being ruined by water sucked up into your vacuum chamber. How does this happen? If you forget to empty your drain bucket, the drain hose will suck up the water when you open your drain valve. This easy to install kit

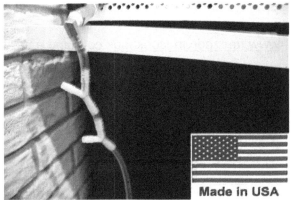

Made in USA

eliminates that problem. The first time you ruin a batch of food, you will wish you purchased one of these.

Freeze dryer Upgrade kit- This kit will eliminate 3 of the most annoying things about the freeze dryer. The bumper pads will stop the acrylic door from hitting the metal cabinet of the freeze dryer. The Hose Grommet slips easily over the drain hose and then slips into the space cut out of the side panel. This eliminates the hose to metal friction and holds the hose into a sloped position for better draining. The 4 shims can be placed under the front feet of the freeze dryer during the defrost cycle. It gives the vacuum chamber a slight tilt that will stop pooling of water in the chamber and stop water from dripping down the front door or onto the floor.

Freeze Drying Cookbook- This comes as an online version that is updated several times a week at www.freezedryingcookbook.com and a hardcopy version with 100+ recipes that can be found at

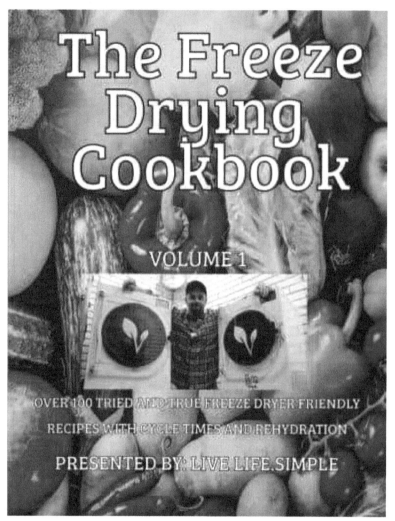

:https://amzn.to/3Y0L2LB or www.freezedryingsupplies.com

All the recipes are specifically tailored for freeze drying using ingredients that will store properly and have rehydration methods. This is the first of its kind, and the first of many volumes we'll keep putting out for you.

Chapter 5

How Long Before I Make My $$ Back?

In some cases, a freeze dryer costs an entire month's wages for someone and the biggest question to be answered for those folks is how fast I can make my money back. If you are diligent and motivated, the quick answer is fast!! How quickly your purchase is made back will depend on your freeze drying purpose and journey. The benefits of the freeze dryer may shine in different areas for different folks. One thing to take into consideration is the cost of running a freeze dryer. I was pleasantly surprised that each load costs me anywhere from $1-3. My electricity bill runs about a $20-25 difference. I run my freeze dryer about 3 times per week. One of my very early videos covers how fast I can make my money back. **Here's the link** https://youtu.be/Tx7vLQiIMCQ I gave three scenarios with 3 types of freeze dryers. This video was filmed a few years ago and the machines are even more efficient now so your results will be even better. The ambitious prepper, the frugal consumer and the enthusiast. The ambitious prepper was able to break even in about 30 days assuming they were freeze drying nonstop. The frugal consumer is a farmer, gardener or savvy consumer that is freeze drying 3 times per week.

They broke even at 13 weeks! This is the user who most matches with the average freeze dryer's needs. **Last, the "average joe"** enthusiast who is only freeze drying 1 time per week was still able to break even in 9 months. When that video was made, the machines were much less efficient and cycle times were in some cases almost double what they currently are.   I would imagine with today's tech and the software getting to increase better over time, it would be much less now. Keep in mind I calculated the 'break even" point as if you were purchasing similar foods commercially for your food storage from big companies like Mountain House, Backpacker's Pantry etc. One big factor that was not factored into this video was the XL size freeze dryer. Output vs. cost, this option would make your money back way faster. For about 25% more cost than the large, the capacity is about 57% more than the large.

For a couple of last resort options, Harvestright also offers layaway and payment options. This is not something that is mentioned on the site, so you have to call in to get this option.   If that's not your thing, people have had good results with pooling funds to buy into a share of the freeze dryer. People do this with their church, family or social groups and get to spread out the investment with good results. The XL size is extra beneficial for this as well because it does such large amounts. If you get creative about buying one and/ or you are committed to food preservation and having a food supply, it's not whether you can afford one, it's that you can't afford NOT to have one. Purchasing commercially freeze dried food or bucket type food supplies are WAAAAAY more expensive. **Don't believe me?** Check out some of my Harvestright vs. videos. We make our own version of a store-bought freeze-dried meals. Not only is it much less expensive, but it also actually tastes good.

How you can BREAK EVEN Faster!!!

Making your money back in 3 months isn't fast enough for ya? Why not sell some of your freeze dried items. Lots of freeze dryers supplement their investment by going to farmers markets, selling on ebay and amazon, even opening store fronts to sell their freeze dried foods and candies. Freeze dried candy has been a trending topic for quite awhile now. The great thing about freeze drying candy is it's very fast and inexpensive. There is little to no moisture in candy, and you can run a cycle in a couple hours using "candy mode" in the newest software. Keep in mind that you will need to adjust a few things like temperature and **physically change to "candy mode."** Candy is also a great way to pay for the foods that you are more interested in having for food storage as well.

Here is a video that will walk you through that software https://youtu.be/WCMkycLPo_g

For more info on CANDY MODE, we will cover a whole CANDY MODE cycle in the running of your first batch section found later in the book.

If you are considering selling your freeze dried foods, make sure you check your local laws for selling food items. Laws vary state by state, even by county or city. Search COTTAGE LAWS for information on this and use the magnifying glass on our Facebook and Mewe groups to search through previous threads.

Chapter 6

My Freeze Dryer was Delivered and Now I'm Terrified.

This whole freeze drying endeavor can be a bit mentally taxing, but fear not, with this book, Youtube, social media groups and lots and lots of other resources, you've got this! The biggest obstacle in freeze drying is the learning curve. Although freeze drying is gaining in popularity, it's still something that is not commonplace (I compare it to the introduction of the microwave in the 1950's). There is a lot to learn about freeze drying but within 10-20 loads, you will know 90% of what you will ever need to know. The first thing you will want to try is the bread run. This removes that "new freeze dryer smell" from the drum and its components. Things can be a bit industrial smelling at first. This also gives you a chance to verify that your freeze dryer and vacuum pump are working properly. You will also want to clean the vacuum chamber, chamber rack and stainless-steel trays thoroughly with soap and water. You may want to do this a couple of times before you put actual food into the freeze dryer. Try some easy things first or try your favorite fruit or vegetable. The only requirement for freeze drying your first load is allowing somewhere for water to escape from the food. If you are doing something like blueberries, grapes, or cherries, pierce an area for that moisture to get out.

What to expect & overcoming the Newbie State of Shock

If you have done some searching on the Facebook groups, reviews and videos, you may have found people that have had problems with their freeze dryers. Most of these people have had problems within the first week of ownership. Let's be honest, this is very discouraging for new owners or potential buyers to see. Most problems do happen in the first or early stages of ownership, but in my opinion, most can be avoided by simply educating yourself about the freeze dryer, the freeze drying process and familiarizing yourself with solutions to common problems. Just to be clear, I am certainly not discounting the folks who have had lemons or quality issues. As with any consumer product, especially appliances and technology, there are some machines that will get out there that just aren't 100%. Freeze drying at home is still in its infancy and brings a HUGE learning curve to consumers. The more you are willing to learn about the freeze dryer, the more you will be able to solve or troubleshoot anything that is thrown at you. I think that doing some simple freeze dried items like candy, fruits or vegetables for your first few loads is very important. It will get you acquainted with the machine, its processes and they taste good and are easy to rehydrate or eat in freeze dried form. They are also quick cycles that will keep your morale high and give you the confidence needed to try some of the trickier items.

What's in the box?

These items are what currently come with the freeze dryers and may change over time. The first time I opened the boxes that come with the freeze dryer, I was impressed at the quality and amount of all the items.

Vacuum pump- This is usually its own box inside a larger box that has the smaller items. If you ordered the oiled pump, it would come with an oil filter and enough oil to get you up and running. It also comes with a manual. It's there so you will read it, educate yourself on how to fill it, maintain it, what TO DO and what NOT TO DO so that it will give you many years of use.

Reusable Oil Filter– this is a custom-made filtering canister made exclusively by Harvestright. It will allow you to filter your used oil and use it over and over. It also has a nifty thumbwheel that marks when the oil was filtered. It comes with one replaceable filter.

Vacuum pump oil- This will be enough oil to fill the vacuum pump and then some. Make sure you put the proper amount of oil into your pump and DO NOT OVERFILL. There are marks on the pump showing Minimum and maximum amounts. Please read the manual for proper maintenance. We will discuss this later.

Vacuum Hose- The vacuum hose looks like a short garden hose and connects from freeze dryer to the vacuum pump.

Mylar bags and oxygen absorbers- Harvestright literally gives you everything you need to freeze dry besides the food. 50 Mylar bags and 50 oxygen absorbers are included so you can freeze dry and store your food right away.

Mylar bag heat sealer- These seals the mylar bags and makes them airtight. Set the number setting wheel according to the mil type bag you are using. Harvestright's bags are 7 mil.

<u>Stainless steel trays-</u> Depending on which size freeze dryer you have, you will get 3,4,5,6 or more trays. These are nice quality, but I highly recommend getting at least 1 extra set.

Chapter 7

Setting Up Your Freeze Dryer

So now that you have a pile of freeze dryer stuff, let's get it put together and get freeze drying!
I have several videos that can also walk you through this.

Here are a few: https://youtu.be/5nWDMbIuIXY

https://youtu.be/ns_JXQ06Kak

The first thing you will want to do for set up is have your freeze dryer in its permanent location. Once it's set up, it's not very easy to move. Next locate the power cord and plug it into the back of the freeze dryer. On older models, it will have two plugs and it can be confusing as to which should be used for the freeze dryer and which should be used for the vacuum pump, but HR made it a no brainer now. Next, pull out the valve on the left side of the freeze dryer (if you are looking at it.) Most of the time, the drain valve is pushed back into a hole on the left side to avoid damage during shipping. Pull it out as far as it will go and attach the clear plastic tube to the end of the brass fitting. This is where the water will drain from the chamber when the freeze dryer is defrosted.

Next, figure out where you want your vacuum pump to sit. It needs to be within a few feet of the freeze dryer. I like to put mine in an area that can get some air circulation. Once you have that set in its place, find the vacuum hose and check to make sure that it has rubber o-rings in the fittings at either end. You can skip to the troubleshooting area in the book if you are not sure what I am referring to. If you have verified those are present, thread on one end to the fitting on the vacuum pump (hand tight only) and the other end on the right side of the freeze dryer (hand tight only). It is important that this hose is only hand tight. You will not need to use pliers or any tools to tighten it. Now plug the cord for the vacuum pump into the back of the freeze dryer and turn the power switch on to the vacuum pump. If installed correctly, the vacuum pump WILL NOT turn on. If it does turn on, you have the power cord plugged into the wrong slot or it is plugged into the wall. **Either way, it's** not right. The freeze dryer will tell the vacuum pump when to turn on by supplying power to that outlet in the back. **Don't panic if your freeze dryer is on** and your pump is not. The pump will not turn on until later in the freeze drying process.

The next part pertains to oiled pump users. If you have the oil less feel free to skip ahead. After you have all of that properly installed you need to add oil to your vacuum pump assuming it is not already filled. Sometimes they are shipped filled and sometimes they are not. Either way check that it has the proper amount of oil to avoid damage to your pump. If the pump was jumbled around in shipping or in transit, allow the oil to settle before running it. If you need to add oil, unscrew the demister (looks like a car oil filter) and add the proper amount of oil recommended by the manufacturer and then screw it back on hand tight. Last, make sure that your gas ballast is turned to the "open" position.

Next double check that the rack inside the freeze drying chamber is firmly plugged into the outlet at the back of the chamber. Also, double check that your rack is put in the right way and not upside down. The orange heat pads should be on the top of the rack (if you slide the trays into the slots, the heat pads will be above the tray and not sitting on rubber) Once you have done that, make sure that the rubber seal on that seals the chamber to the clear acrylic door is properly seated. If you have an older freeze dryer, your setup may include a door pillow. This is placed inside the rubber door gasket. Just be sure that there are no parts of it pinched in between the gasket and the door. The pillows are a bit of a hot topic in the freeze drying community. Harvestright eliminated them because they were deemed unnecessary and not very beneficial. They can be a little bit more efficient and helpful with condensation if used properly. However, I have found that it's nice to be able to see into the chamber when in use and it can also be a place for bacteria and smells to collect so I ditched mine long ago.

When all this has been completed, turn the switch on the back of the freeze dryer to the on position. After 3-5 seconds, the Harvestright home screen will appear! I think you are ready for the first run. The best way is to ease into freeze drying and a bread run is the perfect way to do that.

Bread Run? What the heck is that?

Now that you have been patiently waiting for the components and oil to settle after delivery, and you have put everything together, you are ready for your first load. Many refer to this as the "bread run" and if you have searched through our social media, you have probably seen it referenced. The bread run is no more than placing sliced bread onto your trays and running an entire cycle. Although it is not necessary, it serves a couple of important functions. It will help remove that "new freeze dryer smell". That's not a good thing. Oftentimes, even after a good scrub down, the oil, grease, and new parts put out a specific smell. It will go away after a short time. Most times after you run a bread run. The bread soaks up all that industrial smell just like a sponge. Another very important reason for doing the bread run is to ensure that your freeze dryer is hooked up properly and functioning the way it should. The bread run is very quick because there is not much moisture in bread but will still go through all the different individual cycles. FREEZING, VACUUM FREEZING, DRYING and then FINAL DRY. Depending on the software version being used in the freeze dryer, these may be different but accomplish the same thing. If you are having issues with the freeze dryer vacuum not operating properly, refer to the step-by-step vacuum troubleshooting sections found later in the book.

BEFORE your first load

Before you do your first load, I want to save you some time. I have done probably close to 1,000 cycles now and I have a pretty good idea of what WILL freeze dry vs. what WILL NOT freeze dry. In short, DO NOT do high sugar, high fat or high oil in any form! It will not store and will be a waste of your time. Some of the things that are not recommended will make it through the freeze drying process but will not make it long in storage. I have included a quick list of dos and **don'ts** but if you are uncertain, visit our Facebook group and use the search bar BEFORE you try to freeze dry. Also, just because your favorite recipe has an ingredient on the NO list, doesn't mean you can't modify it slightly to get it to work. Check out the freeze drying friendly ingredient substitution page found later in this book. Some individual ingredients can also be ok if mixed into a recipe or done in small quantities.

DON'T Freeze dry	DO Freeze Dry
Honey	Fruits
Syrup	Veggies
Meat fat	Meats
Oil	Low fat dairy
Peanut Butter	Eggs
Butter	Ice cream & some candy
Nuts	Low fat or low oil leftovers.
Chocolate (in most cases)	Herbs/ flowers
Heavy cream	Pastas and grains
Bones	Marshmallows
Mayonnaise	Seeds and soil

Some easy first things to do:

- Strawberry slices, apple wedges (dip into a diluted lemon juice water to prevent browning).

- Cheese (shredded)

- Leftovers are easy, just make sure they are not full of butter and oil

- Veggies like broccoli, carrots (most are best if blanched first)

- Sliced mushrooms

- Candy such as skittles and taffy are simple and done in 2 hours.

Freeze Drying Raw Foods

My general rule for freeze drying raw foods is to only freeze dry things raw that you would eat raw normally. For example, cook your potatoes before you freeze dry. Raw meat can be done, but I personally **don't do raw meat**. It is too easy to contaminate other foods and easy to forget what is raw and what is not raw. That's not to say that you cannot freeze dry raw meat, plenty of people do it and have great success. I do recommend that if you are going to do raw meat, mark and label very clearly, clean your freeze dryer thoroughly after a raw load and do not mix raw and cooked food in the same load.

Chapter 8

Doing Your First Freeze Drying – Step by Step

First things first, choose something simple for your first batch. Diced fruits or vegetables are an easy one to start with. You want to get in the habit of pre-freezing your food in a deep freeze if you have one. If you **don't, no** big deal, your cycles will take a bit longer. Get your food ready on your trays, just be sure not to overfill them. I like to keep the food under the lip of the tray, at least until you are a little more experienced.

I know before you press that start button, you have an overwhelming feeling of nervousness. We have all been there, but I want to assure you that the freeze dryers made now are intuitive and mostly hands off. Harvestright has had so many people giving data and feedback over the years, that thanks to the 1000's of "guinea pigs' ' who freeze dried before you, the product the freeze dryer produces now is top notch and at this point, virtually unbeatable. Not even the commercially purchased products will be as good as your home freeze dried food. The next pages will walk you through all of the options and settings screens as well as an entire freeze drying cycle step by step.Ok. Let's get started.

Depending on the software you are using, this may be slightly different. Also, as time goes on and software changes, these options may change slightly. If you watch some of my older videos, you will see different prompts and screens. Keep this in mind while watching and reading. **Let's get started!**

Turn the switch to the on position and you will notice the screen come on. The screen is a touch screen, and this screen is how you will navigate the different options. Make sure you have followed all the setup steps and you have everything hooked up correctly. Ensuring you have followed the setup process correctly will prevent you from having a bad first experience and although the software is simple, it is possible to cancel a load mid-cycle and possibly have some minor difficulties.

Starting at the Home Screen

You will see the home screen with the Harvestright logo. In the upper right you will see something like v5.1.19 or a similar series of numbers and letters. This series of numbers and letters is the version of the software you have. You may want to upgrade later when there are updates or if you ever have an issue and you need help, the software version you are using is often helpful to a tech or a fellow freeze drying helper. Updates are available at the Harvestright website when they are available, but I tend to wait a little bit to install the newest software. Many times, there are bugs that get worked out in the coming weeks after a release. If you need to install software, there is a USB port on the right side of the LED screen. You would need to insert a thumb drive into the USB while

the machine is off and then turn the freeze dryer on. You will see a loading screen and if the software updates correctly, you will notice a different "v" number or version number in the upper right-hand corner.

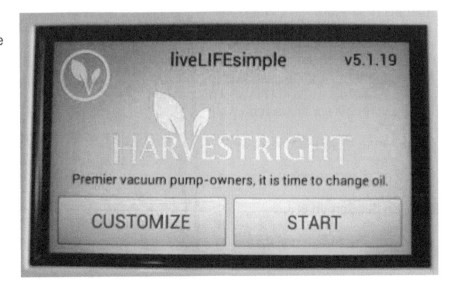

If you ever need your log files for tech support, this same thumb drive process is used.

In the upper center you can hold down the default screen name and change the name of your freeze dryer.   Choose wisely :)

In the upper left corner, you will see a leaf logo. If you press this, it will take you to the functional testing screen that allows you to manually turn on and off the different components of the freeze dryer. You can do this for freeze (refrigeration), heat (your orange heat mats on the rack), vacuum (will turn on the outlet that your vacuum pump plugs into) and an auxiliary relay (for future gadgets?). To turn any of these on or off, just press the tab under the component. The functional testing screen also shows the temperature of your trays, as well as the room temperature. The last thing on this screen is the pressure. For freeze drying, the measurement of vacuum is

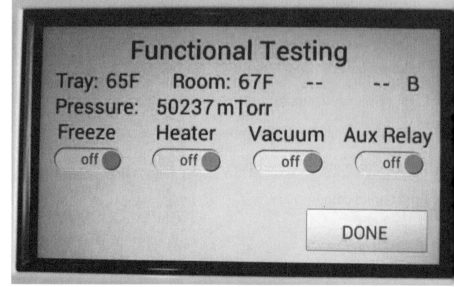

measured in mTorr or millitorr. We don't need to get too technical here but the lower the better. If you ever need to do a vacuum test, this mTorr reading is very important. You can read more about this in the troubleshooting vacuum section later in the book.

Let's get back to the home screen by pressing DONE. If you press and hold the Harvestright logo there is all kinds of useful info about your freeze dryer including: Last time and date of a cycle, Hours of use, batches completed, Pump hours, the serial number of your freeze dryer, your type of pump (for reminder notifications), a choice between fahrenheit and celsius, and whether or not you want the pump to continue running after your cycle is complete. At the bottom you can set your time and date as well (this will take you to a new screen).

If you hold down the pump type area, it will take you to a screen that allows you to choose the type of pump you have and whether you want to reset the reminder notification.

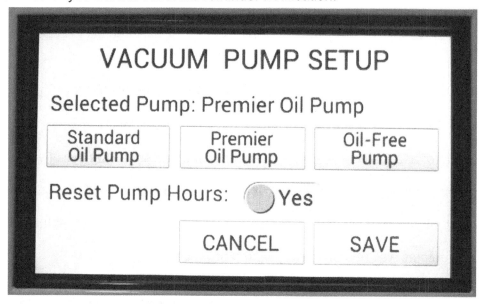

Now go back to the HOME screen and press the button that says CUSTOMIZE. In this new screen you can adjust the temperatures for each part of the freeze drying cycles. To be completely honest, I do not adjust any of these unless I am doing candy. If you want to do candy and your software is v5.1.19 or higher, you can adjust your dry temp to 135 or higher and you will enter candy mode. I will touch on candy mode later in the book. If you do want to change anything on this

screen, click SAVE otherwise you can reset, and you will always go back to default settings.

The only other option on the HOME screen is Start. If you are ready for this, I can guide you through your first batch. LET'S DO THIS!!!!!

Press Start and the machine will then prompt you to wait 15 minutes before adding your food.

You are now ready to add your food. If I have pre-frozen food, I usually add it before the 15 minutes is up since it is colder than the freeze dryer. This screen will also ask you to check that your drain valve is closed.

The drain valve is the valve located on the left side of the machine. It serves two purposes: when closed it allows the chamber to hold a vacuum by sealing off air and when open, it will also be the valve that allows your melted ice to drain at the end of a cycle. If you forget to close this valve, you will not be able to freeze dry and you will get a vacuum error. When the cycle is completely done, once that valve is opened, it will introduce air back into the chamber and then allow melted ice to drain into a container or bucket.

I always pre-freeze my food. I will leave it up to you whether you pre-freeze. I like to pre-freeze for many reasons. The very first thing the freeze dryer does is cool the food down to a very cold temperature. I believe mine is usually around -20 or -30. If you pre-freeze your food, it is already at the freezing temp of your freezer or deep freeze (most likely around 0 degrees.) Your refrigerator freezer or deep freeze is already cold and in use, why not capitalize on that? When your food is already frozen when added to the freeze dryer, it reduces your cycle times and in turn, puts less wear and tear on your freeze dryer and vacuum pump.

In the freezing mode, the machine goes into a super freezing state that will bring the food temp down to around -40 degrees. This is why it is so important to pre-freeze your food in my opinion. If your food temp is already at 0 degrees (instead of room temperature) when you add it in, then the freeze dryer doesn't have to do that part. If you are starting your food at room temperature or still warm from cooking and your freeze dryer is also at room temperature, it will take much longer for the food to

get to the -40 degrees. If you don't pre-freeze, the freeze cycle can take 10-20 hours and if you do a pre-freeze, it will take 3-4 hours. In the long run, not pre-freezing costs you more money because it takes extra electricity. It's also putting unnecessary wear on your freeze dryer and making you wait longer for your food to be done. If you really want to maximize your efficiency in your cycles, pre-freeze multiple sets of trays of food. That way, you have trays ready to go as soon as the previous cycle is complete. If you have tray lid covers from www.freezedryingsupplies.com you will prevent freezer burn and they also stack, so you can stack 4,8, 12 or more trays on top of each other in a deep freeze. When you pre-freeze, it also allows you to store up leftovers and extra food until you are ready to start freeze drying.

Before we get back to our cycle, I want to mention that unless I am doing high sugar foods like candy or ice cream that can melt, I never adjust temperature settings for the freeze dryer. In fact, I wouldn't recommend messing with any of your settings at first. Later, after you are comfortable with the freeze dryer, you can try to play with settings, but 99 out of 100 times, I don't touch it. The freeze dryer is designed to be intuitive and really does all the work for you.

Once you have let the machine cool for 15 minutes, the screen will let you know that it's time to add your food. Press continue and you will go to another screen.

During this time, the freeze dryer goes into a hyper freezing state mentioned earlier, that will take the food's temperature to -20 to -40 degrees. This process will vary greatly depending on if you have already frozen your food, the thickness of the food and the texture type of the food you are freeze drying. If you have frozen your food prior to adding, you will notice a dramatic difference in this cycle time. Typically, the FREEZING cycle will take 4-8 hours, sometimes more (over 12 hours in the picture above) but with pre frozen foods it can knock off 3-4 hours in the overall load time.

You may also notice a screen that says VACUUM FREEZING and the pump will turn on in conjunction with the refrigeration of the unit. This helps speed up the cycle to get the food down to those extreme negative temperatures.

The next cycle is the drying cycle. You will most likely not notice any changes in the freeze dryer noise or function other than the screen changes. During this DRYING process, the actual lyophilization process is happening. Again, you will **not notice a difference of what's happening** with the machine, but inside, the orange heat pads are slowly warming the frozen food under a heavy vacuum and turning the moisture in the food into a gas. That gas is then frozen to the sides of the vacuum chamber in the form of ice. You will notice a large swing in temperatures on the screen during this cycle and gradually the mTorr (mT) will decrease.

The DRYING cycle is oftentimes the longest part of the whole process. Depending on the software you have, you may see a progress bar as well. This is just using a combination of vacuum pressure, temperature, time and some other variables to give an indicator of how far along you are in the freeze drying process. If the pump has not already turned-on during VACUUM FREEZING, then the pump turns on and will run until the cycle is complete. During the drying cycle, you will notice the temperature of the chamber going up and down. This is where the freeze dryer will adjust from hot to cold many times under vacuum. This will turn the moisture in your food into a vapor. You will notice during this process that a layer of frost or ice will form on the sides of the vacuum chamber. The ice is the moisture that has been removed from your food.

Once the mTorr level has maintained below 500 mTorr for a specific period, the freeze dryer senses that there is less resistance and will go into its final dry mode. The mTorr is the number that can be seen at the corner of the screen. In simple terms, the mTorr is a very small pressure measuring unit.

Once the software has determined that the food is nearly complete, the last screen FINAL DRY will appear. This screen will have a 2-hour countdown timer for completion of the batch. This unfortunately is the only way to get any idea of when the freeze dryer will be done. The good news is you are almost done! The

bad news is, this can happen at 2 a.m. or while you are at work. The freeze dryer will hold the food in a holding pattern inevitably until you remove it, however, the sooner you can get to that food, the better. At some point, that food will start rehydrating slowly and undo what you just waited so patiently for. I like to use a bluetooth security camera pointed at the screen. This allows me to check

on what's going on at all times. I have been at the store or a 2 hour drive away and been completely

aware of what's going on with the freeze dryer. The one I use can be found at

https://amzn.to/3hhN8XG   and is easy to use and relatively affordable. The way I see it, the first time

you ruin a batch of food, you could have purchased the camera.

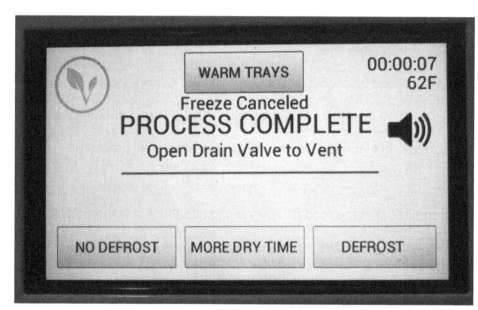

Once the freeze dryer is complete you will see this screen that says PROCESS COMPLETE or something similar.

It will have 4 options Warm trays, No defrost, More dry time and Defrost. DO NOT PRESS ANY OF THESE

OPTIONS! Why? Because if your food is not actually done and free of moisture, you will most of the

time have to start all over from scratch. Unless you use my hack below. I'm not sure why there is not

a BACK button or a PICKUP WHERE I LEFT OFF option, but there needs to be. Harvestright if you

are listening, we need this! I do have an easy hack for this just in case you accidentally cancel out of

that screen.

Hack For Adding Extra Dry Time

Step 1- Start a new batch from scratch. It will take you to the cooling screen again. Press the blue leaf at the upper left corner and it will take you to the next screen.

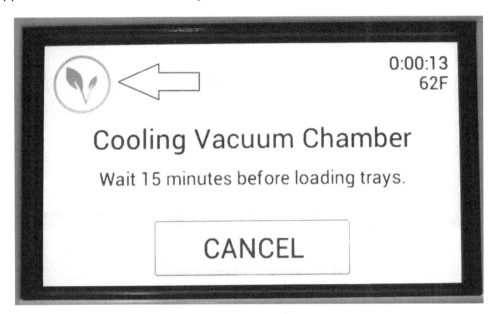

Step 2- By pressing the blue leaf, you will bypass the "cooling" screen and go straight into the "load trays" screen. When you press continue on this screen, it will then take you to the "freezing" screen.

Step 3- Once you get to this screen, you can press CANCEL to get you right back where you started!

Step 4- Here we are again. Press ADD MORE DRY TIME and finish your freeze dried food.

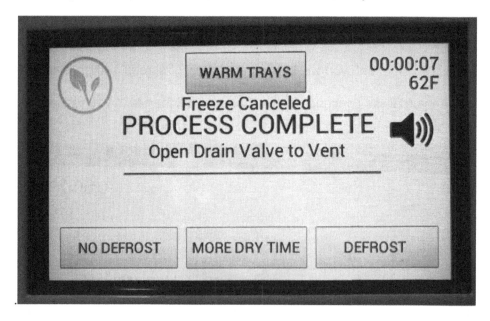

This is not the most convenient way to add dry time, but it does the trick!

Again, if you are not sure whether your food is completely free of moisture, DO NOT PRESS ANY BUTTONS. So how do you know if your food is free from moisture? We will cover all of that later in the book, so for now let's assume it is and carry on.

Finishing your freeze dryer cycle

To determine whether the food is complete, you will need to release the vacuum of your chamber. Turn the valve on the side of the machine slowly and introduce air back into the chamber. Maybe I'm a little paranoid but I let the air back in very slowly. It makes me cringe a little when I see people open the valve all the way and hear the cracking and popping of that super cold steel chamber being introduced to warm air again. Once the vacuum is released the seal on the door will loosen up and you can then open it.

Now let's go over the options on your PROCESS COMPLETE screen. If you have determined that the food is not completely done, you can then press the ADD MORE DRY TIME option and add the desired amount of time. I usually add 2-4 hours. If you want to be certain that your food is 100% dry, there is only one sure way. At the end of the cycle, weigh your trays. Note the weight and place them back into the freeze dryer. Add more dry time and at the end of that time, weigh again. If the weight is less, the food was not dry the first time. Repeat the adding dry time process until the two weights are equal. Most of the time, with most foods, additional dry time is not needed, and you can just feel and see that the food is complete. However, if you are freeze drying thick or dense foods, you may need to add time.

If you have determined that the food IS done, you will need to select a choice on the PROCESS COMPLETE screen. You will have the option to WARM TRAYS, NO DEFROST, ADD MORE DRY TIME or DEFROST.

WARM TRAYS is a function that I never use. There are a lot of opinions on what it is used for, but personally, I don't see the point in warming the trays. If your food is cold and the trays are not warm to the touch or at least room temperature, you need to add more dry time instead.

NO DEFROST is a way to defrost the chamber only using the room temperature. If you are in no hurry to use the machine again, this can be a good option. The room temperature is warmer than the chamber, and after several hours the ice in the chamber will melt and go down the clear drain tube in the side of the machine. Make sure you have a bucket or container for the water to go into or you'll end up with a wet floor puddle or soggy carpet!

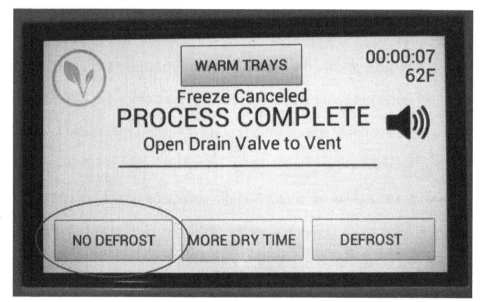

During the defrost process, one of my pet peeves of the freeze dryer happens. There is a drain in the back of the freeze dryer where the melted water goes. If it gets jammed with ice, it will back up and push the water out the front of the chamber onto your floor. If you have some shims or something to wedge under the front feet, you can usually avoid this. Sometimes this will happen even if the drain does not jam up. Our upgrade kit includes some shims to help with this as well as some other fixes.

When the freeze dryer is defrosting, the water will go down that drain we discussed earlier. From there it will go past the vacuum valve and into a clear straw. You will need to have a bucket, container or even a floor or sink drain for this water to go into. While we are on this subject, we should mention that once the chamber is defrosted, you should either make sure that you empty your drain bucket or purchase a "no suck kit" at www.freezedryingsupplies.com

If you don't do one of the above options, you run the risk of completely ruining a future freeze drying load. Let me explain. After you have run an entire freeze drying process, your last step is to open your valve and release the vacuum in the chamber. When this happens, air is being pushed back into the vacuum chamber. That air comes from the clear hose that drains into your bucket. If your bucket or drain container is full of water, it will suck up the water instead of air. This will blast water all over your vacuum chamber and rehydrate your freeze dried food. If you have the "no suck kit" we sell, it allows air to be sucked in but also allows the drain hose to be sitting in water just in case you forgot to empty it.

If your freeze dryer is not going to be used for awhile after this load, make sure that your acrylic door stays propped open to avoid bacteria, mold and smells.

The ADD MORE DRY TIME option is used if you have determined that the food is not completely done. You can press the ADD MORE DRY TIME button and add the desired amount of time.

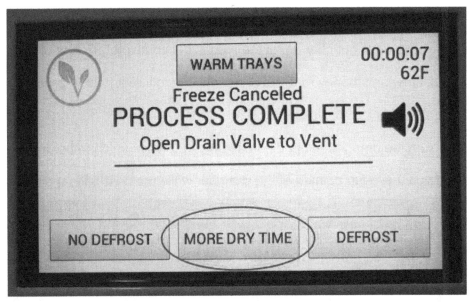

Additional dry times required will vary greatly depending on many variables. I usually start with adding 2-4 hours of additional dry time and determine from there. Check into the section found later in the book on determining if your food is moisture free for more pointers. You will use "Add more dry time" if your food is not completely free from moisture. The goal here is ZERO moisture, no exceptions. It is also important to point out that it's not possible to "over dry" or "over freeze dry." Although there is no surefire way of knowing your food is completely free from moisture, there are some helpful things that you can use. We will discuss these in depth later in the Food Storage 101 section. The easiest way is using 2 of your 5 senses. Touch the food and if there are thick areas, break them in half and feel them. You can also feel the trays when they come out of the freeze dryer. If they are cold, you need to add time. You want the trays to be warm to the touch. You can also use your sense of sight. Fully freeze dried food will usually look different than something that needs more dry time and if there is any moisture present, there will be spots on the tray that are a different color.

This is when I have found the thermal camera and infrared thermometer discussed earlier to be helpful in finding the temps of the trays. The thermal camera and infrared thermometer can get a reading in the middle of food. The ideal temperature for food that has just completed the cycle should be 65-100 degrees + or -. If the thermometer drops significantly in one area, or there is a spot that is still below freezing temperature (30's or lower), then you need to add more dry time.

The most reliable and most certain way of zero moisture in your food is to weigh the trays. Take the weight of your trays, add more dry time and weigh again when that extra dry time is complete. If the weight is less, you still have moisture that needs to be released. Once your weight is the same before and after, you have removed all the moisture. Add dry time if needed, and if in doubt, weigh and repeat until the weight does not change. If the food is not completely freeze dried, not only will you have wasted food, time, and money, but you can get extremely sick from improperly freeze dried items.

The DEFROST button will turn the orange heat pads on and melt the vacuum chamber ice at a faster pace. I have found that if you use a fan pointed at the chamber while the heat pads are on, it will speed up the defrost time immensely. When you circulate the heat, it will defrost the chamber in 15-20 minutes. This means that you can have another load ready and start freeze drying again

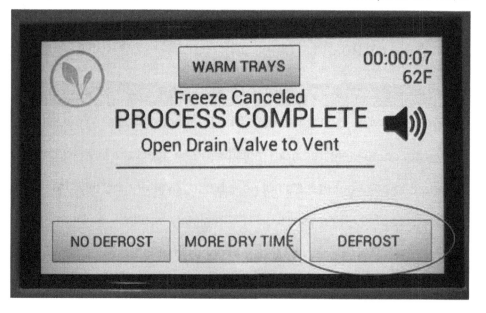

very quickly. Depending on your software version, you may or may not have a countdown clock for the defrost. If you do have a countdown clock, you can adjust the time the heat pads will remain on.

YOU DID IT!!! You have completed your first full freeze drying cycle! I can assure you that each cycle going forward will be easier and probably teach you about the process of freeze drying.

What to do in a Power Outage

One last scenario is in the case of a power outage. This does not happen often where I live so it took me 4 years to figure out. I panicked when it happened because I had the freeze dryer running but I quickly figured out that the freeze dryer can pick up where it left off during a power outage. There is a watch style battery backup on the back of the touch screen that saves the info from your last cycle. If the power goes out, it knows what was going on to freeze dried food right up to the minute. Once the power returns, it shows the number of power outages on the screen and picks up where it left off. Pretty cool. It achieves this from a watch type battery that can be found on the back of the screen. At some point, it will need to be replaced.

Candy Mode

If you are still intimidated, let's do something easy! You can try some simple fruits and vegetables, or we can try the easiest thing there is: CANDY! If you have CANDY MODE, we can go step by step on how to freeze dry candy. Candy Mode is a super fast and super easy way to do your first freeze drying cycle and getting over your newbie paralysis.

Turn on your freeze dryer and at the home screen press the customize section of the screen.

This screen will allow you to change the different settings, but for candy mode you need to increase the dry temperature to 135 or greater. Doing so, the screen will automatically change to candy/ high temperature mode. 135-140 degrees is just fine for most candy, but it can be adjusted all the way to 150 is needed. Click SAVE on this screen and it will redirect you back to the home screen with a small difference on the screen.

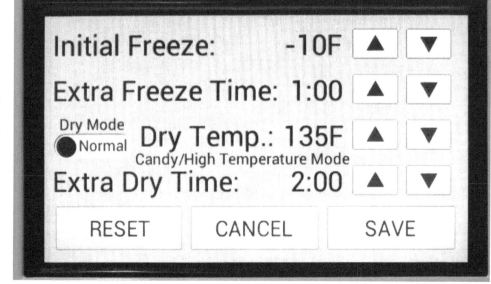

When you return to the home screen it now says High Temperature Mode and it's ready for a candy batch. Press start and the machine will start cooling for 15 minutes.

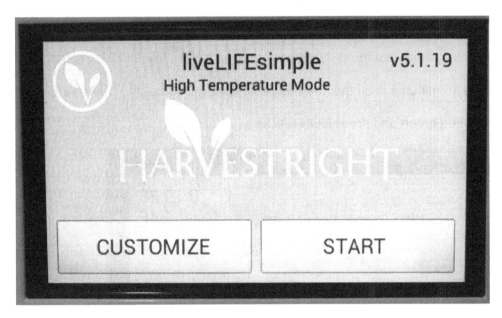

The cooling screen will stay on until 15 minutes has passed. This allows enough time for the chamber to get cold. While you are waiting for the chamber to cool down, it's a good time to prepare your candy.

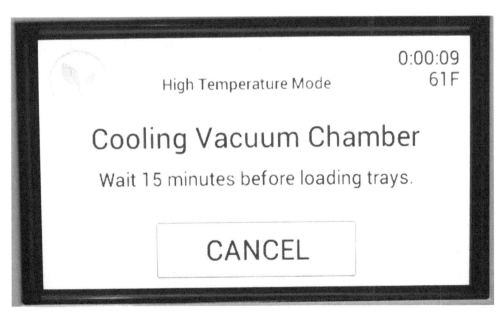

Make sure you leave plenty of room in between pieces because they will expand. Some expand a lot! I always use pre-cut parchment paper when doing candy because it will stick. The dividers set into the 40-portion spacing is also very helpful for almost all bite sized candy because candy will not stick to them, but the dividers will keep the pieces from sticking together.

When the 15 minutes is up the "load trays" screen will come on. Make sure the touch switch is turned to "On" and green and press CONTINUE.

That will take you to the "warm trays" screen. Most candy benefits from a small warming time to soften it up. We often do skittles, nerd clusters, taffy and caramel apple suckers and they all do better with warming the trays 5-8

minutes. You can check the Facebook or Mewe groups for the best practices on certain candies or visit www.freezedryingcookbook.com to see our recipes. If you click skip, it will take you straight into freeze drying. If you click start, it will ask you how long you want to warm trays.

Once this screen appears you can adjust the warming time up and down. If you press CANCEL, you will have to start all over again.

Once the warming time has expired, the freeze dryer will go directly into DRYING mode.

The DRYING mode time will be set to the time that was set in the customize screen at the beginning. For everything I usually do, 2 hours (the default) is plenty of time. If you didn't set it for the time you need, you can also adjust it up or down on this screen. Once the drying time has expired, you have a similar screen as the regular freeze drying process. What is neat is that you can go right into the next candy batch. Candy has little to no moisture so there is no need to defrost between batches. The chamber is already cool, so you can do back-to-back loads. This means a whole lot of candy in a small amount of time!

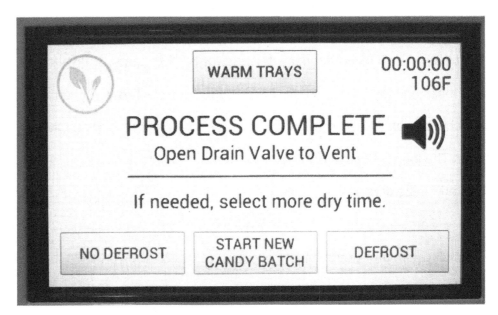

Chapter 9

Food Storage 101 and 3 Things That Ruin Freeze Dried Food

Now that you have successfully freeze dried your food, you need to make sure that it is stored properly. In this section, you will learn about how to seal or store your freeze dried food and what causes food to expire if not stored properly. This is probably the most important section of this entire book because if you do not store freeze dried food properly, you might as well not start freeze drying at all. One of the most common questions people have been HOW LONG WILL MY FREEZE DRIED FOOD LAST? Although there is not a clear answer, the most common answer you will hear is 20-25 years. Scientists have found food from hundreds of years ago that was preserved. Archeologists have found "hardtack" rations from the Civil War and preserved honey in Egypt from the ancient Egyptians. So, if stored properly, the answer is 100+ years. I have food that is well over 5 years old that looks and tastes like the day it was freeze dried. I like to rotate my freeze dried food to reduce my chances of failure. If we are going to use some of our food supply, I try to start at the oldest stuff first. The longer I freeze dry, the more knowledge and skill I have that I did not have when I first started freeze drying.

Some food storage bag companies claim their bags to be 100 year bags. I think that's a little gimmicky. I'm pretty sure that no one will live to 120-130 years old to get a return on their purchase. Guess the following generation will just have to wait and find out. Although our freeze dried food may not last 100 years, we can pretty easily get 20, 25 or 30 years. There are several factors to getting this to happen including the type of food, the makeup of the food, proper freeze drying and most important the way it is preserved once freeze dried. The following info will help you have the best results.

First, you will need to determine the length of storage time desired. If you are only storing short term for personal use or giving freeze dried food as a gift, then the next sentence may not be as relevant to your situation. The 3 worst enemies of Freeze Dried food are:

1) **Light**

2) **Moisture**

3) **Oxygen**

The reason these 3 things are so detrimental for food storage is because those 3 things are needed for bacteria, organisms and fungi to grow. The introduction of one or all these components can alter the flavor, texture, appearance and nutritional value of your food. If this is a product that you desire to reach maximum storage longevity, you will need to eliminate them.

1) **MOISTURE -** If you introduce any amount of moisture to your freeze dried food or the food you are trying to store is not an absolute "0" moisture level, the clock is ticking for the end of shelf life. Also, be mindful of your storage location. Just because your food is dry immediately after freeze drying, a humid climate or damp basement can affect storage time. It is also recommended that your freeze dried food be stored at least 6 inches off the ground. Concrete and floors can hold moisture and also introduce other undesirables to your food. To ensure your best chances of having a "0" moisture level, keep reading below for additional practices.

2) **LIGHT –** Light does not contaminate food. It can, however, reduce the quality of nutrition and taste of food. Light can be avoided by storing your freeze dried food in Mylar bags followed by storage in an area that does not regularly receive any light

(natural or man made). 5 mil and 7 mil Mylar bags are capable of blocking all or a high percentage of light if they are true to their claimed specs. (See Mylar 101 for more information on this) Keep in mind that ball jars will not block much, if any light (see more info below). Mylar bags are not all created equal, and I encourage you to do your due diligence, especially before purchasing a large amount. At www.freezedryingsupplies.com we sell 5.5 mil Mylar food grade bags that are created by a United States food bag manufacturer. They make many of the bags that you see on grocery store shelves as well. We are not the thickest or the least expensive, but the bags are USA made and made by a reputable food storage bag manufacturer.

3) **OXYGEN -** When oxygen gets into your freeze dried food, it causes oxidation. Oxidation is the cause of loss of nutrition in foods, organisms and fungi to thrive, off colors/flavors & oils and fats will go rancid. The two most effective ways I have found to remove oxygen in large amounts and trace amounts are with oxygen absorbers and a chamber vacuum sealer that can seal thick Mylar bags. In most cases, a 300cc oxygen absorber is enough to eliminate a satisfactory amount of oxygen in Mylar bags filled with contents, up to a 1-gallon size. Do not assume this is a one size fits all scenario though. Always consult the manufacturer of the oxygen absorber for recommendations or if in doubt, toss in an additional packet. If you are storing in a bag larger than 10 x14 or 1 gallon size, consult with the manufacturer to get recommendations. (See oxygen absorbers 101 for additional information). ALWAYS use an oxygen absorber for storing freeze dried food in Mylar or food storage bags! NO EXCEPTIONS.

As for vacuum sealers, I have only found a handful that will remove a useful amount of oxygen under vacuum, as well as sealing or double sealing the thickness of Mylar bag needed for long term food storage. I prefer the Avid Armor USV32 and the Avid Armor ES41 Euro Series because they have the ability to do large size (10x14 or 1-gallon bags) and they can also DOUBLE seal the thickest 7 mil bags. If you use a vacuum chamber sealer you still need to use an oxygen absorber! The chamber sealer is removing the volume of air and oxygen, but trace amounts of oxygen can still be left behind. The oxygen absorber can take care of that and in most circumstances. There are other brands out there that are fully capable of doing these things, but overall price vs. functions and quality, these are the best in my opinion.

If you would like to get 10% off a chamber vacuum sealer or any other products from AVID ARMOR, you can follow this link https://avidarmor.com?aff=43 and enter the code **LIVELIFESIMPLE** into the promo code area at checkout.

Rodents

Also, keep in mind that rodents can be a huge factor in storage. I have heard on many unfortunate occasions that rodents have broken through containers or boxes and destroyed years' worth of effort and food. Keep your freeze dried food off the ground in a rodent free environment or in a rodent proof storage container or box. Just because the container is sealed, that does not mean rodents can't get in. They can chew through plastic or squeeze in the tiniest of spaces.

Ball/ Mason Jars

If you are using Ball/ Mason jars to store your food, your shelf life will be dramatically reduced because you are only eliminating moisture and oxygen. Ball jars, even if kept in a dark place, will allow light over time and you will see the food "fade" in color. Another factor to consider when storing in jars is the reliance on a lid seal. Jars and glass are not penetrable by oxygen but ARE completely reliant on the seal. If the seal is not properly seated, defective or just has a very slow leak, you run the risk of adding another component of failure into storage. You can also vacuum seal a mason jar with many different types of sealers and/ or attachments.

How to get moisture free food

If you are not 100% certain that your freeze dried food is free from moisture, oxygen and light, proceed with caution. Foods can look and smell alright but may still be unsafe to eat. Always use your eyes and touch as your first line of defense when it comes to whether your food is done. I also feel more comfortable when the trays removed after a cycle are ALL warm to the touch. As a second line of defense, the thermal camera and infrared thermometer mentioned earlier may help determine dryness as well. If the trays are not warm, add more time. Adding time costs more money in electricity and can be frustrating, but not near as frustrating as a "surprise" when you open a food storage bag or jar, only to find out your efforts have been lost. If you want to be 100% certain your foods are dry, use weight as your guide. When the cycle is complete, weigh all the trays and note the weight. Place them back into the freeze dryer and add dry time. When that is complete, weigh again. If the weights are the same, there is no more moisture to be removed. If the weight went down, place the trays back into the freeze dryer, add time etc. Do this until the weight results are unchanged.

Organizing Your Freeze Dried Food

This is uber important! Especially if you have been freeze drying for a few months. You will quickly notice that your food storage area is filling up. It is very important to get organized and stay organized or you will lose your freeze drying focus. If you get to the point where you no longer have room to store your FD food, you will probably just stop freeze drying. There are several ways to organize your freeze dried foods mentioned here. Find the ones that suit you the best and make a plan.

I like plastic tubs made by Rubbermaid and several other brands. Most of them will stack with each other and they can be easily labeled. If you package them by type of food or date along with a food log and location, you will be able to find specific items when needed. I like these containers for several reasons. They will stack 4, 5, or taller and freeze dried food is lightweight and won't topple over or crush under the weight of the stack. They also hold lots of food storage bags, especially when the bags have been sealed flat or vacuum sealed. If you use these to store mason jars, they will stack 30 jars perfectly with very little extra room. They also block most light as a bonus and can be used over and over.

I currently use catering style shelves for some of my freeze dried food. They are pricey but they make it easy to display your food which makes it easy to locate or sort through. I put the oldest food in the front and newest in the back and rotate them out every year or two if possible. This helps mitigate spoiled or possibly expired foods. These racks can also have wheels on them so they can be moved around if needed. I sort the shelves by food type. My system is types of meats, dairy and cheese, sides, appetizers, individual pantry type items, desserts/ snacks and breakfast. This method works great for me when I want to pack specific meal plans for trips. Being able to see the bags and sort through them is the easiest way I have found so far.

Some people also use a pegboard type system like what you would see in grocery stores or a garage. This method does not offer the most storage, but if you use a bag with a hang hole, it can make a very efficient storage system. If each hanging peg section is labeled grid style (A1, B3, C6 etc.) and then logged according to the food and grid location, finding things can be quick. This also utilizes wall space and not floor space.

One thing that I have learned since purchasing an Avid Armor chamber vacuum sealer is that it makes bags easier to store. It does this by sealing the bags when they are flat and fully compacted. There is no volume of air in them, only the volume of the food. This wastes no space and makes them stack better and neater. It may not seem like you are saving much space in 1 bag, but when you have 100's of bags, it can double your storage space over time. I have been freeze drying for close to 6 years now and have changed my storage type several times over the years. Organization can be a big problem with freeze drying, so make things easy on yourself and plan ahead.

Chapter 10

Mylar Bags 101

Mylar bags are not all created equal. In fact, some "Mylar" bags sold on various sites for a low price are not, in fact, Mylar at all. Some discount sites lead you to believe that the thickness of their bags and the metalized look appears to be Mylar but is actually something else. The true metalization is what keeps oxygen out, not thickness of the bag's core. The word Mylar is thrown around the food storage bag industry very loosely. Mylar is a product that was developed by the DuPont Company and is not actually the shiny or metal looking bags that most envision when they think of Mylar storage bags. The true Mylar is actually clear, and the use of Mylar has become somewhat of a generic trademark such as Kleenex or Chapstick. The addition of an aluminum layer (the crucial part for food storage and freeze dryers) is the part that makes the food storage bag flexible yet strong, and a vital part of making the bag impervious to oxygen penetration. That layer quality is also vital for the effectiveness of blocking oxygen. Be mindful of this when purchasing your food storage bags.

The other major difference between a claimed Mylar bag is the discrepancy of Mil or thickness. If comparing 5 or 7 mil food storage bags, be very weary of the ones that cost significantly less than from a reputable company. Many times, companies will claim a 5 or 7 mil thickness, when, they are giving you the thickness of both sides of the bag added together. For instance, they claim a 7-mil thickness, but each side of the bag is actually 3.5 mil. (3.5 mil +3.5 mil = 7 mil) Pretty sneaky. Another sneaky trick these low-end companies will try is the claim of thickness of bag. They are claiming thicker and thicker bags, but the low quality and thin layer of the aluminum does not protect more. They are only making the core of the bag thicker, not the oxygen barrier. The only true barriers to oxygen are glass and metal.

We sell 5.5 mil food storage bags on www.freezedryingsupplies.com that are true 5.5mil thickness, (on both sides) & made in the USA from a reputable food storage bag company. Ours also have a hang hole built in, they are resealable with a zipper seal, and they are gusseted. Gusseted bags have a built-in flat bottom so they will stand upright by themselves. Whether you purchase from us, or somewhere else, do your research and make sure that you are getting what you are supposed to be paying for.

Mylar storage

If you have been freeze drying for a little while, you are starting to notice a developing problem. You have a limited amount of space for your food storage and your space is going to run out. Here are a few tips for how to organize and how to store Mylar properly.

Mylar organization can be cumbersome. The bags are not a uniform size and vary from bag to bag, even when doing the same contents. They are difficult to stack, and you can't smash them down too much without risking the ingredients poking a whole in the bags or smashing the contents. I have found the first step for organization is to separate foods into categories. For example, meats, loose ingredients, meals, veggies, side dishes, sauces, desserts, breakfast, condiments etc. I prefer an open storage type system if you have the space. If you do not have the space, you will still want to organize by types of foods and then go into storage tubs that are rodent resistant or rodent proof.

Either way, you will also want to be mindful of the age of foods. I find it's important to rotate older foods and therefore, reduce the chances of failed food. Why test the limits if you don't have to?

I realize everybody's reasons and uses for freeze drying are different. I put my food on a combination of shelves, storage tubs and racking. My shelves are organized by food type with the oldest in the front and my newest in the back. A vacuum sealer has been game changing in lots of ways for me and my freeze drying. In organization, it helps immensely. A vacuum chamber sealer removes 99% or more of the air and oxygen from a Mylar bag. If you are strategic in how you place the food into the bag before you vacuum seal, you can get the bag to almost lay flat and it will conform to a more appealing way to stack or store. If you do this over 100's or 1000's of bags, you can easily double the amount of usable storage space for your freeze dried food.

Another handy way to organize part or all your food is to use peg board style organization. You can take a pegboard with storage pegs to hang your bags. I am experimenting with a grid style organization system to locate my bags. Picture the board game Battleship where you call out coordinates to find the opponents location. "B7" is where I would find the Chicken Pad Thai that I made on 7-17-2020. You can then log this into a food log that would give you contents, location, dates, rehydration recipes and other important info.

One last thing to think about for food storage is powdering your contents. Many freeze dried foods can be powdered by running them through a food processor. Lots of foods rehydrate better when powdered such as soups, sauces, milk, eggs etc. The reason I am bringing this up in the storage section is because powdered foods are compact. You can fix several dozen powdered eggs in a quart size bag. If you can fit lots of powdered food in a small space, you have more available room for foods that cannot be powdered.

Mylar bags in addition to properly freeze dried food and the correct steps in removing oxygen have the capability to withstand 25 years or more. Some companies even claim they have bags that will hold up for a century. I don't know about you, but I suspect I'll be pushing daisies by then and 25 years is plenty for my situation. If you want to increase the success rate, you can also put your completed Mylar bags into another container for added protection. Mylar is tough stuff, but it's not invincible to tears, standing water or rodents. Try to keep your stored food off the ground at least 6

inches to help with the above.

How to Properly Fill and Seal a Mylar Bag

To obtain a hermetically sealed environment (oxygen free food storage bag), it must be heat sealed. Mylar can be sealed many ways: A household iron, a hair straightener, an impulse style sealer or a vacuum sealer. In my opinion, the latter options work better and are more consistent. If a person is putting in the work and preparation for food storage, why skimp on the last step? Follow the next steps to get the best possible results for sealing Mylar bags.

1. Label all your bags prior to filling and wait until all bags are full before opening your oxygen absorbers. Make certain that you are using the correct size or number of absorbers (for more info on this refer to the oxygen absorbers 101) section

2. Fill your bags with contents and add the appropriate amount of oxygen absorbers to the bag (see oxygen absorbers 101 for more information on this)

3. If you do not have a chamber vacuum sealer, press on the bag slightly to remove as much unwanted volume and oxygen from the bag.

4. Make sure that you allow enough room at the top of the bag to fully close, make sure there are no obstructions or debris where the seal is going and fully seal the bag. *This could very well be the most important thing to consider. If you do every other aspect of food storage correctly, but the seal does not seat properly or does not get the correct amount of time, the other steps are void. I prefer to double seal my bags just to be sure.*

My Mylar Bags look like they have holes in them! DID I GET A BAD BATCH?

I have seen many threads and comments on our groups and videos concerning "pinholes" "folds" and "see through" areas in Mylar bags. One person even tried to take a picture with a flashlight shining through the "holes" in the bag. Although this seems very concerning and can even put you in a panic wondering HOW MANY OF MY OLDER BAGS HAVE THIS PROBLEM? or IS ALL

OF MY FOOD USING THESE BAGS GOING TO BE RUINED? Chances are, they are fine. The true version of Mylar (the clear part of the bag) is one of the strongest flexible materials known. The aluminum sheeting used in the bags is not. If the bags are bent or creased, it can cause very small pinholes in the metal foil. It does not affect the reliability of the bags for storage, only cosmetically. **Don't believe me?** Fill one with water. Water will travel to the path of least resistance. If you do have a water leak, it might be time to have a conversation with your supplier. If you **don't have a** water leak, chances are. Your food is ok.

Chapter 11

Oxygen Absorbers 101

There is lots of information out there about oxygen absorbers and unfortunately some pretty common misconceptions as well. I have pooled info from many of the largest manufacturers of oxygen absorbers and food storage companies to help understand what an oxygen absorber does, how they work, how to use them properly and how big (or small) size oxygen absorbers you need to use. This information combined with other information on this site, can help you reach the longest-term food storage possible. (See food storage tips and Mylar 101 for additional hints). Oxygen absorbers are considered non-toxic and Generally Recognized as Safe (GRAS) by the FDA because they remove oxygen without chemicals.

Oxygen absorbers (sometimes confused with silica or dessicant packets) essentially trap oxygen in their environment until they have reached their capacity. This is why an oxygen absorber, once opened, should be placed immediately into a food storage bag or storage container and sealed as quickly as possible. If left out too long, the oxygen absorber will reach its usable capacity for absorption, sometimes in 10-15 minutes, and not function properly when and where it's needed. Oxygen absorbers only absorb oxygen (not moisture or air) and will only work as they are intended with fully dried goods.

One of the biggest misconceptions is that a sealed food storage bag should collapse or have a "vacuum sealed" look after the oxygen absorber has been used. You should not feel unvalidated because your food bag does not look vacuum sealed. If you want the vacuum sealed look and benefit, you will need a vacuum sealer that will seal thick mylar bags. The oxygen absorber may reduce some of the volume of the bag, but only eliminates oxygen, not air. Oxygen only makes up 21% of the air inside a food storage bag. Before sealing your bag, you can remove additional air and oxygen by reducing the unnecessary volume in the bag. Try to squeeze, move or reposition the contents to reduce the volume. Keep reading the next section to see how you can increase your chances of removing more oxygen.

What size Oxygen absorber do I need?

Oxygen absorbers are made from iron powder and when exposed to oxygen, become iron oxide. Through this process, the oxygen absorber will remove oxygen in its bag, container or area until it is full. Most oxygen absorber packets you see are categorized by cc amount. This refers to the amount of cc's of oxygen it is capable of removing before it is full. Keep in mind the cc's of oxygen you need to remove is that of the bag or container when filled with contents, not the empty volume of the container or bag. The $1,000,000 question is **what size absorber do I need?** There are many variables that need to be addressed before answering this question with certainty. With the following information and the charts below, you should be able to get a good idea of the correct size for your needs.

The main questions you will need to answer are what type of food you are storing and what size container or bag you are using as well. The type of food you are storing matters because you need to have some idea of how much oxygen the food is holding as well. "CC" stands for cubic centimeters. Most containers are measured in mL, but lucky for us, 1cc is the equivalent of 1mL. The most basic and simple way to figure out the cubic centimeter volume or "cc" is to divide the cc or volume amount by 5 since oxygen is approximately 20% of the air inside the storage container or bag.

In most cases under 1 gallon, 300cc is sufficient. Keep in mind this is a general suggestion and the recommendations made are assuming the container or bag is full of contents or how dense the food is and there are variables that will change the size needed. You cannot overdo the amount of oxygen absorbers used and, in many cases, certain foods like flour or pasta hold 50-75% air so take that into consideration. Another reassuring point to this is an overage of absorber size can continue absorbing oxygen in a bag or jar with a small leak for several years. This means that food that would have, in most cases, been ruined, may be fine after all. Another refreshing fact is that most oxygen absorbers will absorb more than their rating. DO NOT however, try to use this to your advantage. I always encourage freeze dryers to do their own research and/ or consult with the manufacturer of the oxygen absorbers.

Basic Recommendations for Oxygen Absorbers by Storage Size

For Mylar food storage bags:

Quart Mylar (8x12) = 300cc

Gallon Mylar (10 x 14) = 300cc is usually sufficient. However, sometimes 2 depending on freeze dried food type. If in doubt, use 2!

If you are using Mason Jars, the barrier (glass) around the food cannot be manipulated (doesn't shrink in), so the safest way to judge absorber size for a jar is to assume as if it were empty of contents. Here are the recommendations for mason jars.

½ Pint jar = 50cc

Pint jar = 100cc

Quart jar = 200cc

Gallon jar = 800cc

One more way to dramatically increase your results for removing all or most of the oxygen in your storage bag or container is vacuum sealing. I have the best results with a chamber vacuum sealer. This makes the success rate go up by dramatically removing the amount of volume, air and oxygen that you start with. For example, Let's assume 2 people are storing an identical food product. They are both using an identical Mylar type storage bag. They are also using the same recipe and using the same size oxygen absorber. One is using a vacuum chamber sealer and one is just putting the food directly into the bag with the absorber. The person that vacuum seals is not only removing most of the volume of air and oxygen from the space, but is also removing some from the food as well. Oxygen can get embedded or trapped in food and by removing as much oxygen as possible prior to sealing, the oxygen absorber has a far better chance of removing any leftover oxygen, if any. It also makes a leak very visibly obvious if the bag were to get one.

What do I do with extra Oxygen Absorbers?

When you buy oxygen absorbers, they come in packs of 10, 25, 50 and sometimes 100's or 1000's even. The problem with having lots of oxygen absorbers is when you are packaging freeze dried food, you rarely use the perfect amount of bags to oxygen absorber ratio. So, what do you do with those extra absorbers? You can't leave them out or they will be useless in a short period of time. Safe working time is 10-15 minutes, and most absorbers will absorb their full capacity within an hour. There are a couple of options that will keep them good and ready for the next time you are packaging.

The first, is a simple ball/ mason jar with a known working lid. I like to place the color indicator that comes with the absorbers in the jar so I can keep an eye on that as well. The indicator is a small piece of plastic and paper that in most cases, reads pink if the absorbers are working and purple if they are not. If you have a mason jar sealer for your vacuum sealer or food saver device, you can use that in addition to ensure that the lid is sealed and extra air volume and oxygen is removed.

The second way of storing unused oxygen absorbers is to place them into a Mylar food storage bag and seal. I prefer this method only if you are not planning to use them for a while. This method works just as well as a jar but is a little more tedious and not as convenient. I also try not to waste Mylar bags, as they are expensive and while you can reuse them, you lose a little of the usable bag area every time you cut it to open it. I have also re-sealed the plastic bag that the oxygen absorbers come in using a impulse sealer or vacuum chamber sealer. Set your heat seal low and experiment with which setting works the best. It can melt the plastic bag if it's set too high.

You can also greatly increase your chances of successful oxygen absorber storage by placing them into a vacuum chamber sealer. This removes most or ALL the oxygen while in storage and can be done with a jar or a bag.

At www.freezedryingsupplies.com we sell oxygen absorbers in packs of 10 to reduce the amount that needs to be stored and the potential for waste.

How do I know if my oxygen absorber packets are "good"?

So, you just purchased a bunch of oxygen absorbers and you are ready to use them. Before you add these to your hard-earned freeze-dried food, make sure they are fresh and ready for use. Follow these tips for optimal results.

1. A new packet of absorbers should be vacuum sealed (no exceptions).

2. There should be a color indicator inside the packet. Before you open it, make sure the indicator is the correct color. For most, that would be pinkish/ red. If it is purple, they are no good. Sometimes they can have specks or spots in them. If they do, allow them to sit in their new environment for a few days before chalking them up as "no good." Also consider using this indicator if you are repackaging your unused absorbers. (For more info on this, go to "What do I do with extra oxygen absorbers?" section mentioned earlier.

3. A "good" or "fresh" oxygen absorber should feel pliable, and the contents will feel loose like if it were filled with flour or powder. If it's hard or crunchy, it's probably not any good.

Chapter 12

Freeze Dryer Maintenance

"If you take care of your freeze dryer, it will take care of you."

Like most things in life, you get out what you put in. How does that apply to your freeze dryer? A freeze dryer is a simple, yet complex appliance that needs to be running at peak performance for the magic of lyophilization to happen. That means your understanding of how to keep all the components clean and functional will guarantee that you have a freeze dryer that lasts a long time with minimal hiccups along the way. The great thing is that maintenance is quick and simple for the most part.

How to clean your freeze dryer vacuum chamber

The first time that you have a food explosion, bubble up or freeze dry a load of Carolina reaper hot peppers, you will need to clean your freeze dryer drum. Even though the freeze dryers are built to a high standard out of high-quality components, they do have some sensitive materials in them. This means that you need to be mindful of what you are using to clean your machine. Not only that, but you also need to be mindful of what you are using around your food.

Mr. Clean is a no no. Windex, nope. I think the best thing to use for cleaning all parts of the freeze dryer is good ol' soap and water with a little bit of elbow grease. For those youngsters out there, that's not a brand of grease, it means "hard work." You may also want a soap with an antibacterial or something to kill bacteria, mold etc. but minimally abrasive. Also, make sure that you are using an unscented soap, so you don't end up with fall breeze flavored freeze dried apples.

I have, in the past, used vinegar, vodka or clear liquors and rubbing alcohol, but you must keep in mind that rubber (on the door seal and heat mats), acrylic type plastic (for the door) and even stainless steel, can deteriorate over time. That means you want the least possible chance to do that. I have a video on this topic that you can check out at: https://youtu.be/THp4-Vsc4vY The step by step of cleaning the vacuum chamber or "drum" is straight forward if you know what you're doing. That's where this tutorial comes in.

When, and I do mean when, you need to clean the vacuum chamber, you first need to pull off the black rubber door gasket. There is just a groove in the back that sits over the rough edge that protrudes from the chamber. While you have the gasket off, run your finger down that groove to check for debris or deterioration of the gasket. Once you have done that, wash or clean out that groove with a brush or a q-tip. You may also want to scrub up that whole gasket. The gasket is what makes the seal of the door and the chamber, and if there is anything on there that is not supposed to be, you might get a vacuum error. Try not to use a towel or cloth to dry. It seems like the gasket is a

magnet for dust and debris from cloth. Just let the gasket air dry it for a while.

When the door gasket or door seal is off, slowly pull out the shelf from the vacuum chamber. Before you pull it all the way out, notice that there is a wire harness and a wire going out of the

vacuum chamber. This is a very sensitive piece of the machine, so act accordingly. About 6-8 inches from the shelf, you will see the wiring harness. This allows the shelf to be separated from the vacuum chamber. The easiest way to do this is to set the shelf on something level or slightly below the chamber and using the slack in the wire, set it down.

The wiring harness has a tab that needs to be depressed and then the two connections can be separated. When you separate the connections, make sure that you are holding the connectors and not pulling by the wires. The way I see it, if you can do your cleaning without disconnecting, that would always be the best option, but let's face it, an explosion of food that has been heated is usually

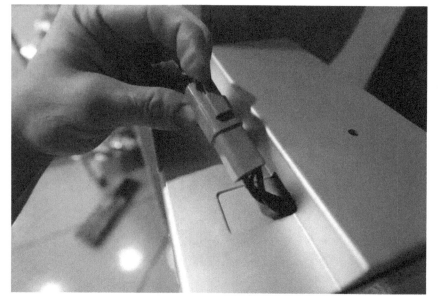

stuck on surfaces pretty well. It usually takes a good scrubbing to remove.

Once the shelf is outside the chamber or disconnected, you can clean the drum itself. I have found this bottle brush https://amzn.to/3RJjRD6 on Amazon to be inexpensive and fit perfectly in between the shelves for scrubbing. If your chamber still has some cleaner or water left in it, open your drain valve to drain any cleaners or water left. A Lot of folks use this time to clean the drain tube

as well. They tend to get food, mold and particles built up inside the hose over time. Some people use brushes and cleaners, just keep in mind what we talked about earlier. The parts can deteriorate over time, and this is also an area that is near your food. Now that your vacuum chamber is clean, let's put it all back together!

Make sure that your chamber and shelf is dry and free from cleaners and soap before putting this all back together. They will be around or in direct contact with your food. To put the shelf back into the chamber, set it on the same pedestal that you used to take it out and plug the two connections back together. The next part can be tricky until you get the hang of it.

There are a few feet of extra wire to allow the shelf to be disconnected, however, when you are putting the shelf back into the vacuum chamber, it can get bunched up and not allow your shelf to slide all the way to the back. The easiest way that I have found to do this, is to take the slack in the wire and place it on the top of the shelf while sliding it in. As you get farther back, let as much slack out as you need until the shelf has hit the rear of the chamber. You **will know** if it's all the way back because there will be some space in front of the shelf. Now you can install the door gasket back on. If the gasket does not go all the way on, your shelf has some wire stuck behind it and the door will not fully close. Once everything is back together, close the door and make sure you are getting a good, visible seal all the way around the gasket.

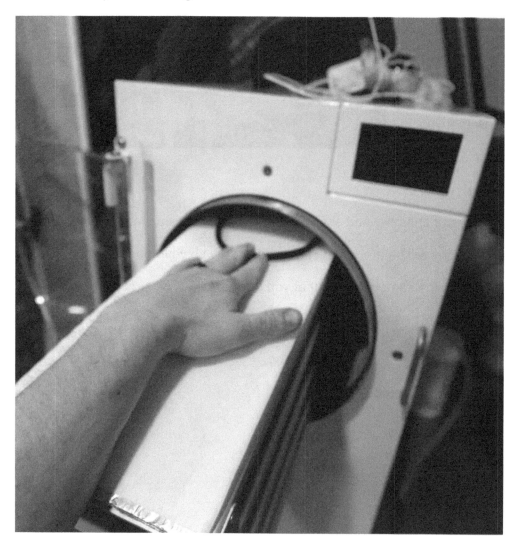

Oil Change Message

When you first purchase your freeze dryer, it may ask you what type of pump you are using. This information is used for the machine to set a reminder at certain intervals. These intervals are preset to the machine for the number of cycles done or hours on the machine. If the message comes up in error or if it's not set right, there is no need to panic. The machine is not directly communicating to your pump, it's only basing this message on those preset intervals.

You can select pump type or reset the message by going to the home screen and pressing the HARVESTRIGHT logo. It will take you to a screen that shows lots of information about your freeze dryer, including which type of pump you have. Press the pump area and it will then take you to a screen where

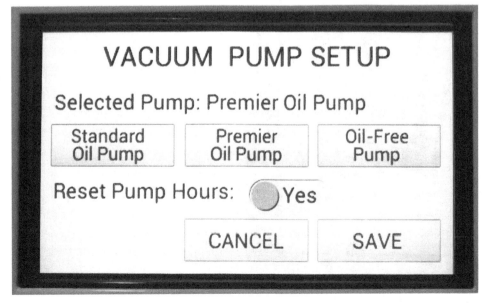

you can change the pump type and reset the message. Click save and you are ready for your next freeze dry!

Changing the Oil in the Vacuum Pump

This used to be the absolute worst part of freeze drying. I swore off freeze drying a few times over the years (very temporarily) because of it. On the early versions of freeze dryer pumps, the oil had to be changed every single cycle. You should feel like the luckiest freeze dryer alive that you now only must change your oil every 20-30 cycles. The old pumps also collected water that had to be separated from the oil regularly. The pumps are also way easier to do an oil change on than they used to be. This is a brief tutorial on how to change the oil on a premier pump. Things may look slightly different on your pump, but generally, things will be similar.

If you want to view a video tutorial, follow this link https://youtu.be/U2aeRTMhvac

Over time, this book may date itself as well, so your best bet is to refer to your user manual or consult your manufacturer. Oil flows the best when HOT, so if you can do this right after the pump has been running, your oil will flow faster and tend to get more crud out.

Step 1- I prefer to place my pump about 1 foot off the ground or on a pedestal. Place it just above the container or filtering system you are draining into.

Step 2- Find your drain plug, make sure it's over the drain container and twist or remove it. Oil will immediately start flowing. If you have the filtering system from Harvestright, there is plenty of room in

the top reservoir to hold the entire contents of the vacuum pump. It will take several minutes for the oil to stop and when it does, I like to tip the back up to get that little bit of extra out. It seems like the worst stuff likes to hide in that last bit of oil. Your sight glass window should be clear, and oil should not be visible.

Step 3- Remove the demister canister at the top of the pump. It looks like a car oil filter. If you have an older pump, you may not have one, but you will have another plug instead. Whether you have a demister or a plug it will be threaded and will need to be unscrewed to reveal the oil fill area.

Step 4- If you have a small funnel that fits into this oil fill, I recommend using it. Some brands of vacuum pump oil have small pour spouts on the bottle that are also helpful for pouring. Make sure your oil drain plug is closed at this time and start filling with oil. The premier pump will take less than 1 quart of oil, so fill slowly. Pay attention to the sight glass while filling. When the sight glass starts to register oil, slow way

down or stop and allow it to catch up. Oil travels slowly into the pump and once you start to see it on the sight glass, there is more coming. Once it has caught up, keep pouring until you reach the desired amount on the sight glass. On the premier, I usually fill right in between minimum and maximum. I have heard conflicting arguments for the proper fill mount, but the best bet is to follow what the manual says. The latest versions may change from what is written in this book.

Step 5- Always check the oil level when it's cold and on a flat surface. If you check the oil right after the pump has been running or has a slight tilt, your reading will be inaccurate. If you have too much oil or too little oil in the vacuum pump, the results can be catastrophic for your pump.

Step 6- If your oil level is at the desired amount, thread the demister or fill plug back onto the pump and you are ready for your next freeze dry! If you are filtering your oil, go to the next section and we will discuss how to filter!

How to Filter Your Oil

An important or possibly the most important thing you can do to ensure a long life of your vacuum pump is keeping clean, water free oil in the vacuum pump. The included filter with your freeze dryer makes filtering easy and does a pretty good job of removing water from the oil as well. That, in conjunction with keeping the ballast on the vacuum pump open (if it has a ballast), can lengthen the life of the vacuum pump greatly. (Ballast in the "open" position pictured)

If you notice that your oil is cloudy or chunky, it needs to be filtered immediately. If filtering does not remove the cloudiness, discard the oil. The oil becomes cloudy when it has food particles in it, or it has some amount of water in it. If you neglect to filter the oil, the internals will start to corrode and eventually get damaged to the point that they no longer work. An easy way to separate water from oil is to freeze it. The water will freeze, and the oil will not. Once frozen, you can just pour off the oil and the frozen water is left behind. Filtering the oil with the included oil filter is so fast and easy, that you really have no excuse to skip it.

I prefer to filter or change the oil when it's warmest and right after I have completed a freeze drying cycle. When the oil is warm, it moves much faster and doesn't stick to things on the inside. It makes it easier to get as much oil out of the vacuum pump as possible. I tend to sit the vacuum pump on a pedestal or something that raises it above the height of the filter. This way the oil can just drain straight into the filter. Let's go through a quick tutorial.

Before we release the oil, make sure that your oil filtering canister has a filter in it. Open the drain plug with the filter lid open. The reservoir of the filter should hold more than enough oil from the pump to prevent overflow. It can take several minutes for the vacuum pump to completely drain so I usually just let it go while I am packaging food or doing something else. I like to get as much oil out of the pump as possible. The grimy oil tends to hang out at the bottom of the pump and it's not unusual to see big globs of stuff come out at the end.

Once you have gotten a satisfactory amount of oil out of the pump, close the drain plug and put the filter away from a potential spill scenario. The filtering process can take quite a while (sometimes even days) and will not happen before your eyes. If the filtering process is taking days or many many hours, it may be time to change the filter or check for big clogs.

The oil has been successfully filtered when it's transparent or you can see through it. If you can't see through it, you can try filtering it again. You will notice that filtered oil is no longer clear like it was when it was new, but more of a brown color. That is normal and remember you are looking for transparency, not color. If you can't get the oil transparent with a 2nd filtering or it has already been filtered multiple times, it's probably time to discard the oil. If you need to discard your oil, I have found that most Auto stores will take any type of oil for free, including vacuum oil.

Cleaning the Freeze Dryer Internals

Just like your refrigerator, your furnace or electronics, you will need to clean the inside of your freeze dryer at some point. The vented panels on the sides of your freeze dryer are usually a good indicator of how much dust and dirt are being sucked up into the inside. You may also experience longer cycle times and a dirty condenser and/ or refrigeration unit may be the culprit.

In order to clean the refrigeration components, you do need to remove the side panels. That can be a task but there are usually about 20 screws (depending on which generation freeze dryer you have) that need to be removed. You can see how to remove panels in the *vacuum error troubleshooting* section found later in this book. The panels are relatively straightforward to remove, and I find that the better you know the freeze dryer and how it works and how it's put together, the more in tune you are with the process as a whole.

Once you have all the panels off, I use either compressed air or a vacuum to get the coils and components clean. A soft brush or duster can also be helpful. The freeze dryer tends to run hot and if the inside components get full of dust bunnies, it has a harder time moving air and keeping cool. Use caution when cleaning because there are sensitive and delicate area in there. Watch for loose wires and electronics and while you have the panels off, try to familiarize yourself with the parts of the freeze dryer and what their function is. If for some reason you need to maintain the freeze dryer in the future, this will help you in being comfortable with what to expect. If you are ever in the situation that something is not working and you must pull off the panels for the first time, chances are you will be frustrated and not want to familiarize yourself with freeze dryer parts in that state of mind.

The Importance of Oil in the Vacuum Pump

The vacuum pump is the heart and soul, the workhorse, the lifeblood of the freeze dryer! It's also the achilles heel of the freeze dryer. If your vacuum pump is not working properly, you are at a stand still. If you have the oiled pumps, there are lots of things that one can do to increase the longevity of them. First and foremost, the quality and type of oil is the MOST important thing you can do. If your oil is dirty with contaminants, water and debris, it cannot do what it is designed to do. The oil serves many functions in the pump including keeping the pump cool, collecting undesirable contaminants and sealing parts to maintain a vacuum. I use Robinair premium oil in my premium pump. It has always served me well and it is a quality oil for the cost. There are plenty of good quality alternatives as well. DO NOT IN ANY CIRCUMSTANCE use Dairyland oil in the premier pump. Dairyland has detergents in the oil that separate water and oil and the premier pump cannot get rid of the moisture in the oil like it is designed to do. I have heard from various sources that Dairyland is fine to use in the Standard pump and the old JB Eliminator. I personally have used and tried Dairyland in the past on older pumps and I do not care for it. It does a great job keeping the inside of the pump clean and separating water, but it added a funky taste to some of my freeze dried food. I don't know why, and I don't want to know why, anything that adds off tastes to my food is not going near my freeze dryer.

Cleaning the inside of your Vacuum Pump

Please note that by following this procedure you are doing so at your own risk. This is how I do this process, but there may be different or other recommended ways of doing it. If this is not the manufacturer's way of doing this, it could potentially void your warranty.

If you have the oil less pump, other than a dry flush after every batch or every few batches, there is not much you need to do other than a rebuild every couple thousand hours. The dry flush and recommended bearing maintenance intervals have changed through the years. So much so that I can't keep up. Search the Retired at 40's freeze drying group on facebook to see what the latest maintenance interval is. There are lots of knowledgeable people on there, as well as some Harvestright techs. Simply put, keep moisture out of this pump or it will not last. The oil less pumps do not take the same measures to dispel water and moisture as well as the oiled pumps. Another suggestion is to keep the oil less pump above where the vacuum hose goes into the freeze dryer. This can help moisture from getting into the pump.

If you have an oiled pump, you can do the maintenance yourself. If your pump is working properly and the oil looks relatively clean when changing the oil, I would not recommend cleaning the internals until necessary. The premier pump and even the older standard pump are very good at keeping contaminants out of the oil. They are also very good at keeping water out of the oil and therefore keeping the interior parts of the vacuum pump clean. If you are seeing chunks, particles or lots of water during your oil changes, you may want to consider cleaning the internals of the vacuum pump. Water and foreign debris can cause the inside of your pump to corrode and eventually cause something to fail. This is a messy job any way you look at it, so you will want to do this outside.

Step 1- Drain every bit of oil out of the pump that you can. The more oil you can get out of the pump, the less will end up somewhere else. Follow the directions in the *Changing Your Vacuum Pump Oil* section from earlier. You will also want to remove the demister.

Step 2- Depending on which type of pump you have; you will need to separate the oil reservoir from the pump itself. In every vacuum pump I have seen the pump and motor are located on the back, and the reservoir is on the front. There may be different models available in the future, so please keep this in mind. Next, locate the bolts (most are 4mm) that are holding the reservoir to the pump and motor. There should be one every few inches around the outside of the reservoir (like a car oil pan.) Slowly loosen all bolts just enough to allow the reservoir to separate slightly. **You don't want to** completely remove the screws.

Step 3- Once the tension has been removed place the pump upright like the picture and gently pull apart the reservoir from the motor casing. There is a seal in between these that can be fragile, and you do not want to break it or have to replace it unless necessary. If you do not have a replacement seal, you will not be able to freeze dry until you get a new one. DO NOT PRY OFF THE COVER! You may have to gently tap the reservoir with a soft mallet to detach the seal.

Step 4- Once the seal has been broken, you can remove the bolts fully and fully separate the reservoir from the motor housing. You may want to do this over a garbage can or put down some cardboard during this step because most of the remaining oil will come pouring out at this point. Allow the two pieces to sit for a while to allow the oil to completely drain out.

Step 5- Once the oil has drained, remove large chunks of debris or corrosion with paper towels and you may need to use a small soft brush. You can also use a cleaner that will evaporate such as carburetor cleaner or brake cleaner. Those cleaners will help loosen up stubborn sections of debris and then evaporate without leaving chemicals behind that may thin the oil. If you want to be certain that there are no oil thinning agents left behind, you can run the vacuum pump after it is put back together and change the oil right after.

Step 6- Make sure when you are cleaning that you are getting all pieces inside the pump. Oftentimes the moving internal vacuum parts are where debris builds up. This is also a good time to clean the oil level sight glass with a Q-tip.

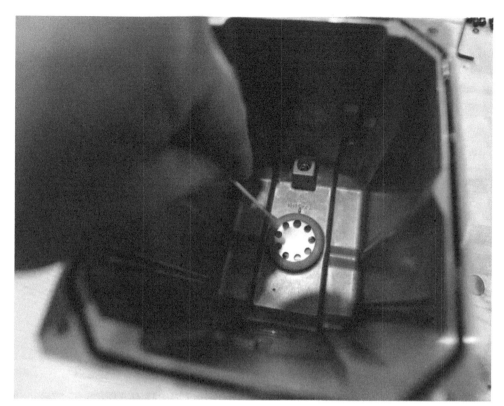

Step 7- When all build up and corrosion has been removed you are ready to put the pump back together. If the seal does not have oil on it still, lightly coat the seal with oil before putting it back into place. This will help seat it and properly seal off the two parts. The seal must be properly seated for the pump to function correctly. The seal holds oil in and allows pressure to build up as well. Before you place the reservoir cover back on, double check that the seal is properly lined up and seated on the motor side and the reservoir side. Tighten the bolts back into the housing but do not fully tighten.

121

Step 8- When you are ready to tighten down bolts, it's important to tighten down evenly and in small increments around the seal. DO NOT FULLY TIGHTEN one bolt at a time. Do a couple of turns on one, then move to the opposite side and do a couple of turns until you have fully tightened all the way around.

Step 9- Fill oil to the proper amount for your pump and test out the pump after it's connected to the freeze dryer. You can manually turn on the pump on the functions screen by holding down the leaf logo on the home screen. Allow the vacuum pump to run until the mTorr level is 300-500 and check for leaks.

Chapter 13

Rehydration Best Practices

The process of freeze drying removes all moisture in foods, flowers, seeds etc. and in order to get the item back to pre-freeze dried, you will need to add the moisture back in. This, (in my opinion) is the most difficult part of freeze drying. Although there are many foods that can be enjoyed in the freeze dried state, some are best eaten rehydrated. Certain foods will only rehydrate properly one way, while others can be rehydrated every way possible. The tricky part is knowing which way works for which foods. The last thing you want is a pile of rehydrated mush.

Rehydrating is introducing liquid back into the food. But there are no rules when it comes to what type of liquid. One of the coolest things to do when rehydrating is to experiment with new flavors and liquids when rehydrating. This can open totally new flavor profiles for your food. Here are some examples:

- *Steak can be rehydrated with marinades

- *Pork can be rehydrated with apple juice

- *Rehydrate breads with broth

- *Rehydrate French toast with butter and syrup

- *Rehydrate fruits with alcohol for a quick drink mixer

This section is one that will continue to grow over time with the increasing number of users and data. The following are all suggestions and intended as a reference when especially trying those tricky or stubborn foods. This is not a one size fits all, so some experimentation may be required. The easiest way to calculate the amount of liquid you need to reintroduce to the food is to weigh your trays (in grams) before you freeze dry and then weigh again after freeze drying. Subtract the after weight from the before weight. You then divide that amount by how many servings you have in the tray and that is the estimated amount of liquid to add. If you use dividers, it makes this easy.

For example: I have portioned my tray with the dividers into 10 servings. My tray of food weighs 1275 grams before FD and 510 grams after FD. The difference in tray weight is 765 grams. I have portioned to 10 servings so each serving will need approximately 76.5 grams (per serving) of water to rehydrate. (765 of water removed /divided by 10 servings). Use the rehydration conversion chart found in the following pages to help with this process.

Rehydration Tools

Vacuum Chamber Sealer - This is my favorite and newest way I have figured out how to rehydrate. You can place certain foods into a bowl or container (one that will fit into the chamber) and add liquid of your choice. This means that you don't have to use water, you can use marinades, beer, broth etc. You can then place the container under vacuum and all of the pores of the food open up. When the vacuum is released, the food sucks up the liquid like a sponge. This can be done with freeze dried or non-freeze dried food and the rehydration is often instant.

Crock Pot/ Instant Pot – Introduces moisture slowly (pressure cooker, Ninja Foodie, Instant Pot) Use the basket that comes with most cookers. This allows the food to remain out of the water at the bottom, but still allows steam to hydrate.

Steamer- Introduces moisture slowly. This allows the food to remain out of the water at the bottom, but still allows steam to hydrate. This can be a slow but effective way for raw vegetables.

Bamboo basket – This is similar to a steamer and introduces moisture slowly. This is a simple wicker-like basket that goes over the top of a boiling pan. The steam from the hot water will slowly add moisture back into the food just be careful not to burn.

Boiling water – Whether you accomplish this from the stovetop or the microwave, this is the easiest and most common way to rehydrate foods. It's also the most convenient. This can be used with a food scale to really nail down a formula for making a consistent finished product. Add some tray dividers to make equal portions and a good freeze drying recipe from our cookbook, and you have the easiest and most predictable freeze dried food!

Ziploc and paper towel– Oftentimes, things that have a bread or cracker-like consistency can be brought back slowly if placed into a zipper bag with a damp paper towel. This allows the food to rehydrate but not get soggy. I place mine in a refrigerator overnight and that is usually plenty of time for rehydration. Sometimes flipping the bread or muffin or whatever you are rehydrating is required to rehydrate each side.

Spray bottle- A small mist from a spray bottle can be helpful for coating the outside of tricky foods with water, but not over saturating them. This can also help spray a layer of liquids onto a food as an adhesive for toppings before freeze drying.

Refrigerator – If the food you are trying to rehydrate needs to be done slowly, but is also susceptible to spoilage if left out, throw it into the refrigerator. The paper towel and Ziploc method is a good helper with this. The refrigerator also has a good amount of humidity in it to help hydrate.

Sous Vide– This could be one of the best kept rehydration secrets there is. Sous Vide can be a wonderful way to slow cook meats and foods in their own juices and spices. It cooks very slowly at a consistent temperature, so the food stays moist and tender. For freeze drying, this means you can add a whole new level of flavor if reintroducing water or ANY liquid to rehydrate. This is an underutilized device that can cook foods in liquids other than water. You can cook freeze dried steak in a marinade or broccoli in broth to add a whole different level of flavor! The result is a tender and tasty rehydrated food.

Pantry Items- We love having lots of loose freeze dried ingredients in our pantry. Freeze dried mushrooms, onions, garlic, cheese, peppers etc. and commonly used ingredients can be stored in mason jars or airtight glass containers. When making recipes like soups, casseroles or really anything, grab a handful of the freeze dried version of your ingredient and let it rehydrate in the cooking process!

Your mouth- Some freeze dried foods take on a whole new life when freeze dried. There are lots of foods that I prefer eating freeze dried over hydrated and they are just best if they rehydrate in your mouth or in your belly. Peaches are my favorite! The flavor is intensified during the FD process and there's no sticky mess!

Wondering what to do with all the delicious food you are freeze drying?

When it comes to reconstituting, *thought and patience are key*. You cannot just dump in hot water and hope for the best. You may be disappointed. **You can always add more, but you can't just take it back** (with one exception below). Here are some tips after almost 6 years of reconstituting.

1. Soups and most stews are very forgiving. Add very hot/boiling water a little at a time until it is the consistency that you want. Let it sit for 5-10 minutes to rehydrate bigger pieces like ham or beef, or simmer in a pot.

2. For items like lasagna slices or a casserole, wrap in a damp paper towel and microwave on a very low setting, steam, or let sit in the refrigerator for several hours.

3. For seafood, use cool water or it will be rubbery or overcooked.

4. Meat, raw or cooked, is forgiving and will only take up what it needs. Use water or broth or add marinade. Too much soaking though can dilute your flavor or seasoning. Taste to see if you need more. It often benefits from time in the refrigerator if the pieces are larger. Shredded cooked meat reconstitutes quickly.

5. Things that are powdered or crushed, like mashed potatoes or mashed squash, or fruit/veggie powders, or tomato powder tend to reconstitute quickly. Add water slowly to avoid over diluting.

6. Most dairy benefits from slower reconstituting in the refrigerator. Milk, sour cream, cream cheese does better with some blending before and after sitting. Cheeses do better grated or shredded with cool water sprinkles, not soaking.

7. Eggs, raw scrambled, do best using cool water and sitting for a few minutes before cooking. There are many posts on the subject for ratios to reconstitute. (Retired at 40's Freeze Drying Group on Facebook and MeWe)

8. **Some things are "gourmet" NOT reconstituted. Cake** slices? Just like biscotti. Feta and blue cheese crumbles? They are great, just crunchy on soups and salads. Desserts and ice cream? Novelty crunchy sweetness.

9. Delicate items like leaves, herbs, spinach, or kale ribbons reconstitute just by adding them directly to what you are cooking, like soup or scrambled eggs.

10. Again, give your food some thought. Pasta and rice should be al dente or it will be mushy by reconstituting. Some things do better by steaming.

11. Final suggestion: When you want to reconstitute, search the group (Retired at 40's Freeze Drying Group on Facebook and MeWe) for your specific food item. You will almost always find someone who did it and got a great result. Try their method until you become comfortable.

Rehydration Conversions

Use this guide when rehydrating foods!

A very helpful way to rehydrate freeze dried food is by weighing the food before and after freeze drying. I prefer to weigh in grams. There is no fumbling with lbs. & oz and to be honest, I'm not very good at math! Grams make converting much easier! Here is a simple chart to help you figure out the amount of water or weight that needs to be used for rehydration. Keep in mind that if you are using a liquid other than water for rehydration, the weight, and therefore the amount needed, may change.

1 gram = 1 cc of water (may not apply to other types of rehydration liquids)

1 Cup Water = 236 grams (varies slightly with temperature)

½ Cup Water = 118 grams

¼ Cup Water = 59 grams

⅛ Cup Water = 29.5 grams

1 Tbsp = 14.7 grams

1 tsp = 4.9 grams

Chapter 14

<u>Freeze Drying Helpful Hints & Hacks</u>

1) *If possible, PREFREEZE! Pre-freezing your food saves energy, saves wear and tear on your freeze dryer and makes your batch times faster.

2) *Keep your freeze drying area well ventilated, climate controlled between 60-78 degrees and use a fan aimed at your pump and freeze dryer to help the freeze dryer run at optimal efficiency

3) *You can also use a fan to speed up the defrost cycle. Circulating the warm air from the heat pads will defrost the chamber in 20-30 minutes. If you can remove the rack, you can pull the ice out sooner than that.

4) *If cooking oily meats or foods, rinse with water and pat oils and fats off with paper towels before freeze drying.

5) *When freeze drying spicy or smelly foods, you may need to clean the vacuum chamber. The spice from peppers and the smell from things like onions, garlic, and chili can linger for several

freeze drying cycles. Instead of cleaning the chamber, I will run my next load of food with something that will compliment the spice or taste, all the while absorbing the smell in the process.

6) *When sauteing, use broth or water instead of oil.

7) *Try adding some carpet or rubber underneath your vacuum pump and freeze dryer feet to quiet it down. Sometimes a reduction in vibration can stop sound from resonating through its stand or cart.

8) *If you get water in your oil, place it in the freezer. Water freezes and oil will not. When the water is frozen, pour off the oil and remove the ice.

9) *When doing raw meats, raw eggs or other contagious foods, DO NOT mix with other foods in the cycle to avoid cross contamination. Also, **don't forget to label bags and anything that these foods come in contact with.** You might remember now, but you might not in the future.

10) *To clean your freeze dryer and plexiglass door, DO NOT use bleach or harsh chemicals, they will deteriorate the glass, rubber seals and heat mats as well as potentially get into your food. Some suggested alternatives would be grain alcohol, Vodka, vinegar, rubbing alcohol but best of all, **good ol' fashioned s**oap and water with some elbow grease. These are just suggestions, please do your own research before cleaning with these. You can also watch this video! → https://youtu.be/THp4-Vsc4vY

11) *You can vacuum seal jars and bags by removing your rack and placing the jar or bag into the chamber. If you are using a bag, impulse seal the top and trim a small corner off below the seal and then fold the bag over and lean it against the side of the chamber. If you are using a **jar, place the lid on** but don't fully tighten down the ring. Press the leaf logo on the home screen and turn on the vacuum pump. Let the pump run with the chamber closed and sealed

130

for 30 seconds or more. The lid will seal and the bag will remain vacuum sealed long enough for you to seal it with an impulse sealer. Here is the link on how to do this

https://youtu.be/i1jLOWmJ36Y

12) *Instead of carrying trays full of liquid to the freeze dryer, you can avoid spillage 2 ways: First. You can set an empty tray in your freezer and fill it. **Once the liquid is frozen, you don't have** to worry about it spilling. Second, if **you don't want** to freeze liquids, just place an empty tray almost all the way into the freeze dryer rack and pour contents directly into the tray.

13) *You can layer your freeze drying trays with pre-cut parchment paper. Place your first layer of **food (let's** say sliced bananas) on the tray, then lay down a sheet of parchment and do another layer. If there is room for the air to flow and moisture to escape, you can double your capacity with certain foods.

14) *If you freeze drying large amounts of things that need to be sliced, try using a food processor, salad shooter, egg mandolin, apple corer or pineapple slicer. These make quick work of commonly freeze dried foods.

For lots of other ideas, helpful products, tips and tricks, watch the HARVESTRIGHT HACKS playlist → https://www.youtube.com/playlist?list=PLFxpwpnn4TgVuVhj9XGRxuIxeNtiTPtN7

For streamlining your freeze drying process and HACKING your food storage, see our products at: www.freezedryingsupplies.com

Common Substitutions for Freeze Dryer "Friendly" Recipes

Mayonnaise:

Plain yogurt, plain Greek yogurt, plant-based yogurt, sour cream (in some cases)

Syrup and Honey:

These have a long shelf life and don't FD well. I like to make packets of them. For example with french toast sticks I packaged some syrup in a sealed packet and put it in the bag with the FD'd sealed french toast sticks (for other ideas See sugar substitutes below)

Sugar in baked dishes:

bananas, Stevia, or (in some cases) freeze dried watermelon powder or freeze dried banana powder are great sweeteners

Peanut Butter:

Powdered PB2 for peanut butter flavor. Can also use Avocado if you just need the "fat" content of the peanut butter for baking.

Butter:

Use Avocado in place of butter when baking (mash or blend for butter like consistency

Oil For Cooking/Sautéing:

Any kind of broth or plain old water. Just add a little at a time as you sauté.

Oil For Baking:

Apple Sauce, Banana, Pumpkin, avocado (cup for cup substitution)

Eggs (Yes, eggs do freeze dry. These are suggestions for vegan recipes):

-Aquafaba (liquid from chickpea cans)

-You can use a quarter-cup unsweetened applesauce for one egg

-Flax Seed Egg: Combine one tablespoon of ground flax seeds with three tablespoons of water for every large egg you need

-Mix a teaspoon of baking soda and a tablespoon of white vinegar together for a light and fluffy substitute for one egg

Heavy Cream:

-Cashew Cream (soak cashews in hot water for 30 minutes, drain, add to blender with a little water. Add water until thick "cream" consistency.

-1 cup milk with 1 to 2 tablespoons cornstarch or flour. (Whisk milk into cornstarch or flour little by little.)

-Cream cheese whisked with a little water

Buttermilk:

-1 tablespoon fresh lemon juice (or light vinegar, such as white, white wine or champagne) to a measuring cup and add enough milk to reach 1 cup.

Chapter 15

Troubleshooting A Vacuum Problem: From Easiest to More Difficult

The dreaded **Inadequate Vacuum Error**……. It stops you in your tracks. There is no convenient time for a vacuum error to occur but hopefully with this troubleshooting tree we can figure out the problem…. **or** at least rule out some others. As frustrating as repairing a freeze dryer can be, I can assure you once you have a fully operational machine, there is nothing like it! We will start with the easiest solutions first and work our way into the more in depth. Please note that some or all these repairs could potentially void your freeze dryer warranty. **If you are under warranty, contact Harvest Right first and follow their recommendations.** If your freeze dryer is not under warranty, any advice you take from this guide is strictly at your own risk. Before you attempt any of these solutions, make sure that your freeze dryer or vacuum pump has not been altered in any way with accessories on the vacuum pump, cooling boxes, in line filters etc. There is a lot of bad information out there that won't just void your warranty, it may be the cause of your problem.

Is it plugged in properly?

Before we get started, make
sure that your vacuum pump is
plugged into the freeze dryer
itself, not plugged into the wall.
(See picture)

The outlet on the back of the
freeze dryer is made for the
freeze dryer is made for the
vacuum pump to plug into. If
your vacuum pump is not

plugged into the freeze dryer, then it will not turn on when it is needed. Therefore, the inadequate

vacuum error will show. This might sound silly, but it has happened to many, many people (including

myself).

You also need to make sure the **switch on the pump** is turned to the "on" position (see picture)

Do you have enough oil?

One thing that is commonly neglected is the correct amount of oil. I fill mine to the halfway point or slightly above. (See picture) Consult your owner's manual for your specific pump and always follow manufacturer's guidelines. When determining your oil level, the vacuum pump should be on a level and flat area, with cool oil. The vacuum pump should also be off (not running). Keep in mind that as you start to run your pump, the oil level will drop (sometimes dramatically). This is completely normal. Make sure that your vacuum pump has fresh, clean oil in it. The pump oil is not only a lubricator, but also a sealant for parts of the vacuum pump and keeps the pump cool.

Is your valve closed?

Make sure that your valve on the side of the machine is closed. The closed position will be a 90-degree angle to the valve (see picture). If the valve is open, your machine will not be under vacuum and give an inadequate vacuum error.

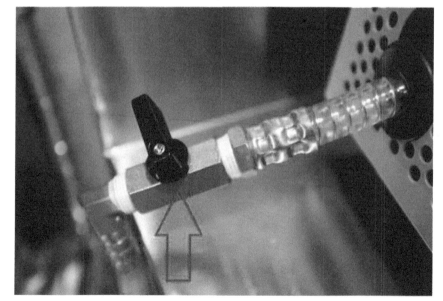

Everything is set up correctly, now what?

If you check all the above and everything is correct, the first step if your pump is under warranty is to download your log files from your machine and get them to Harvest Right. This will help them determine if the vacuum problem is caused by your pump. To do this, get a thumb drive and place it in the USB slot next to your screen. Files will automatically upload. You can also start researching some of these other diagnostics while you are waiting for a response.

Troubleshooting Step #1

The door gasket is the big black rubber type ring that gets squeezed between the vacuum chamber and the clear door. If there is any debris on the outer side or inner side of the ring, it can cause a slow leak. Remove the ring and pull apart the back slotted side apart to check for defects or debris. (See pictures) You can also run a cotton swab or other cleaning tool in the back crevice of the gasket several times to determine if there is an obstruction or debris. This gasket is the easiest place for vacuum to escape so it is best to clean this frequently. The best type of cleaner for all parts of the freeze dryer is non scented, non-abrasive soap and water. Check the front of the gasket as well and clean if needed.

Before putting the gasket back on, ensure that there are no rough spots or debris on the stainless chamber protruding out from the freeze dryer. This is where the crevice of the gasket meets the chamber and if there are any imperfections on the chamber, that can affect vacuum as well. If you notice defects or white strings or threading in the gasket, you may want to consider a new gasket. Another way to be certain that the door gasket is not the culprit is with

some soapy water. Run the vacuum with the door closed and the valve shut. You will start to notice a line where the gasket meets the door. This line should not only be visible all around the gasket, but

as the vacuum gets stronger, that line will get bigger.

Once you have a good vacuum going, pour soapy water at the top of the gasket in between the freeze dryer and the door. If there is a leak, the soapy water will be visible while it creeps its way into the vacuum chamber.

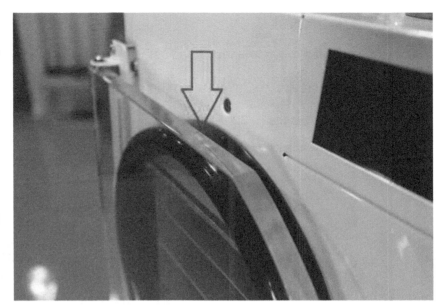

How to fix a gasket leak

To fix the leak, you will need to adjust your door and where it meets up with the gasket. You want the gasket and door to meet as flush as possible all the way around. There are 4 vacuum chamber adjustment bolts (5/32" Allen) as well as the 2 or 4 door adjustment bolts (5/32" Allen).

There is no "sure" method for adjusting these, it will depend on how your door and seal meet. It may take some time to get the right combination of adjustments, but your end goal is to have a snug seal against the door forming a visible circular line where the gasket is sealed. DO NOT OVERTIGHTEN bolts or the door.

Troubleshooting Step #2

The second easiest diagnosis is to remove the hose going from the freeze dryer to the vacuum pump. It is very important that the fittings on that hose are only hand tight and that **no sealant or Teflon tape has been used**. If you used a tool to tighten the fitting or if sealant of any kind was used, remove it or loosen the fitting so it is only hand tight and free of sealant. Once the fitting is loose and unscrewed, examine the O-rings inside of the fittings. They are

typically black rubber gaskets. If there is debris, damage or a break, replace the O-ring. They can be found at any hardware store.

You also might want to check the hose crimps as they can fail. If you suspect that this is the problem, Harvest right can sell or provide you with a new hose or you can use self fusing silicone tape to wrap the crimps. This can be found at any hardware store. Before you reinstall the hose,

also examine the fittings on the vacuum pump and the freeze dryer itself where the hose connects. If there is any movement or looseness, tighten or diagnose what is causing the fitting to move.

There is also an o-ring inside the fitting of the 90-degree elbow. This can fail and cause and leak. The elbow can be found by removing the back panel (⅛" Allen). In newer models, the elbow is integrated into the chamber. The o-rings can be found at any hardware store. If the problem is beyond tightening these or replacing the o-ring, continue to the next step.

Troubleshooting Step #3

PRESS and hold the leaf on the upper left of the screen and you will see a functional testing screen that will allow you to manually turn on and off various parts of the freeze dryer.

(If you have an older version of Freeze dryer, you may not have

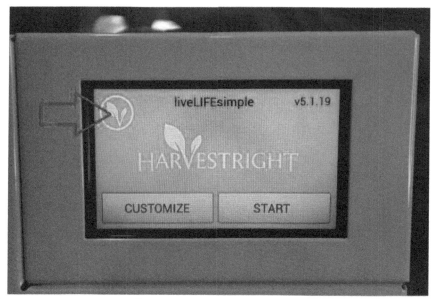

this option.) If you have older software, you can press TEST and manually turn on the vacuum from there. If your Harvest Right is even older, you may not have the ability at all. However, you can still plug your vacuum pump into a wall outlet and do this manually.

To remove as many variables as possible, you will also need to remove your shelving unit. To

do this, remove the black door gasket, slide the shelf out of the vacuum chamber and disconnect your electronics plug. (See picture) Then make sure your valve is closed and close your door. You also need to ensure that the chamber is free of food and / or water.

Close the door and make sure that it is getting good contact and ensure that the pump is plugged into the outlet on the freeze dryer and pump switch is at the "on" position. Make sure that your pump has clean, fresh oil as well. The oil in the pump serves many purposes other than lubrication. It also helps seal parts and pieces for vacuum. (As mentioned earlier)

Manually turn on the vacuum by pressing the touch screen button for "vacuum". (See picture)

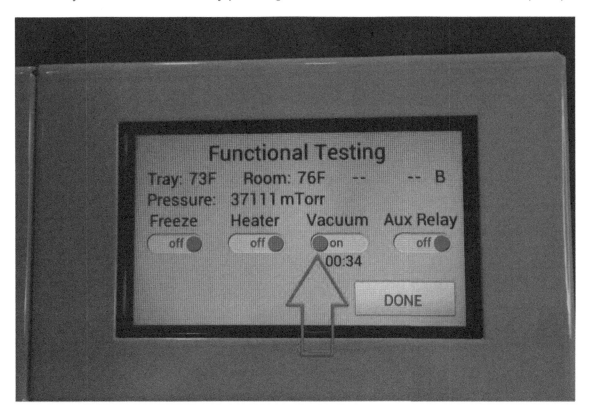

NOTE: this screen is very helpful for many things, not just the vacuum. This screen also allows you to turn on heaters and the cooling system. There is also an auxiliary, I would imagine for future add-ons or diagnosis. There will be a small lag time before you hear the pump click on. Let this run for several minutes and you will see the real time mTorr on the screen. The mTorr will drop rapidly at first and then slowly stop or the number will drop slowly. You are ideally looking for an mTorr below 500.

You should also notice the gasket contact point in the glass will get thicker and look smashed. (See picture) If not, your door is not seating properly to the gasket and could be your vacuum problem. Refer to Step #1 on how to adjust your door as this may solve the issue.

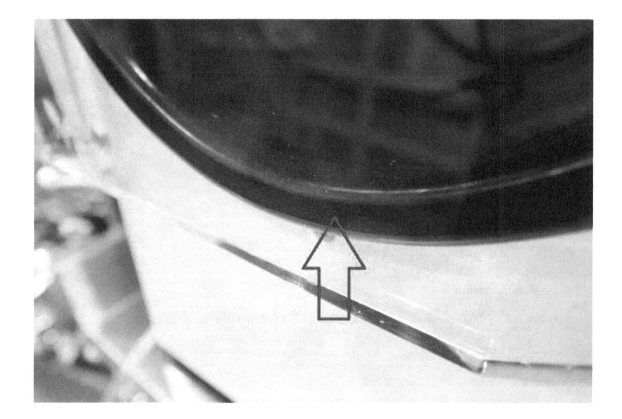

Troubleshooting Step #4

While your machine is still holding a vacuum, the next test will be to determine whether your valve is functioning properly. To do this, fill up a cup or container with water and place your drain tube into the water (see picture). IF YOU HAVE ADDED any anti siphon y's to your drain line, you will need to remove them BEFORE you do this test and put your longer piece of drain line back on the valve connection.

If you have a larger leak in the valve, you will notice water start to creep up the drain tube. It will certainly be the valve because if the valve was functioning properly, it would allow very little or "0" vacuum to escape. The water creeping up the tube (like drinking from a straw) is the valve allowing air back into the vacuum chamber. Let the tube sit in water for at least 1 minute to allow for any

changes. If the mTorr has not changed at all or significantly, remove the elbow or barbed brass fitting along with the tube. (See picture) The next step may help determine whether the Teflon or sealant on the brass fitting is bad or whether we need to keep tracking down the leak.

Troubleshooting Step #5

For the next step, you will need some Windex cleaner or carb cleaner. Remove the brass barbed fitting from your valve. With the brass barbed fitting removed you will have one open

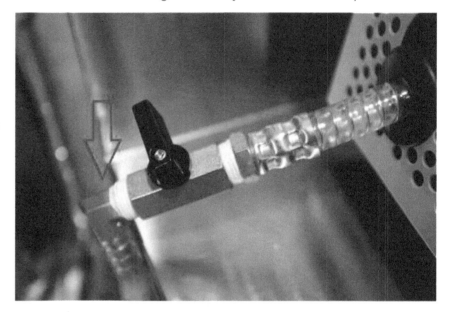

threaded end of the valve showing. Spray Windex or carb cleaner in the open end of the valve as well as the knob or turn switch of the valve (these are usually black). Watch your mTorr level for the next minute. If it has not moved, your barbed brass fitting is leaking. If the mTorr does increase significantly, your valve is potentially bad.

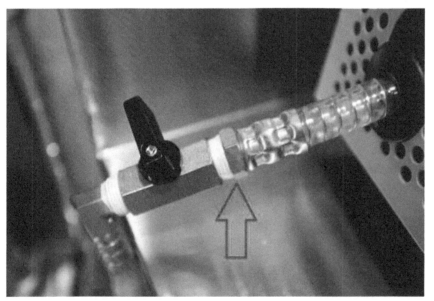

Let's try one last thing before replacing the valve. Spray the other end of the valve (the side that has a hose going into the machine) with Windex or carb cleaner and watch for significant rise in mTorr. If spraying that area causes a change in mTorr, the teflon or sealer needs to be replaced. Also pay attention to the knob and tighten if necessary. In my opinion, these valves are not great quality, and you can find a way better quality replacement at any hardware store. Drain water from the freeze dryer can be slightly acidic and will deteriorate a low-quality valve. Make sure it will handle the pressure of a freeze dryer, but most will be sufficient. If in doubt, and you already have the valve pulled off anyway, I would consider replacing it with a better one anyway. The valve size needed is ⅜" pipe thread, not ⅜" compression.

Troubleshooting Step #6

If you have determined that the valve is fine, we need to keep traveling up the system to determine if the internal drain hose is leaking. Depending on the year and model of the freeze dryer, you may need to remove a cover panel. This will expose the internal drain hose and fitting (see photo). Repeat the same process as earlier, spraying the hose itself with Windex or carb cleaner, the fitting and crimping and watch for a change in mTorr.

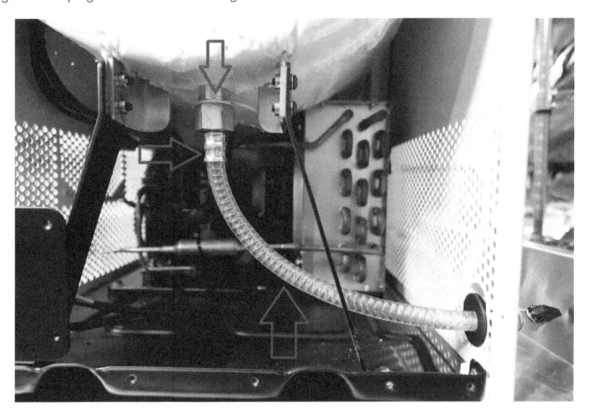

If you find that this is your leak, contact Harvest Right and they can send you or sell you a new assembly. You may also be able to find the parts and fittings you need at a hardware store. The hose is a ¾" size.

Troubleshooting Step #7

If you have made it this far, I feel for you. You are probably upset and have used some choice words about the freeze dryer and your choices. I have some good news and some bad news. Which would you like first? The good news of course because we are staying positive so we can start using this amazing machine!!! The good news is, if you are 100% certain that your vacuum pump is working properly and you have done all these diagnostics, there is only one thing it can be. The bad news. You more than likely have an epoxy leak. The epoxy vacuum feed that seals to the vacuum chamber is not fully sealing and needs to be addressed. (See picture)

You may want to remove the top and side panels to get access to diagnose. Once panels are removed, reinstall your vacuum hose back to the fitting and vacuum pump. Make sure you are using a vacuum pump that is functioning properly. You will also need to confirm that the oil level is correct, the oil is fresh, and your hose is hand tight with no teflon or sealant. You then need to bottom out your mTorr level the same way you have done in earlier steps. Make sure you do all of the same things as removing the shelf and dropping the mTorr level down to its stopping point. Once you have done that, pull back the foam insulation and use carb cleaner to spray the epoxy vacuum feed in various places. There are different versions of how these attach and the overall looks. My version is

a 2022 (pictured)

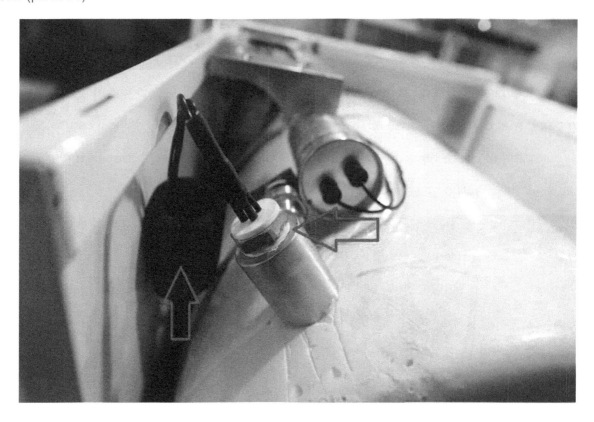

If you see a spike in mTorr levels, you have found your leak. You will need to contact Harvest

Right to find out the appropriate epoxy or I have heard of some freeze dryers using 100% silicone as

well. Please note that if you do not contact Harvest Right before trying this, you will possibly void

your warranty, or they may not help any further.

To repair the vacuum sensor, I must first tell you that this is at your own risk! I am just giving

my opinion on how to do this repair. Any repair that you do at this point is based on your choice to do

so and assumption of your abilities and skill level.

Make a funnel or dam (with masking tape) at the top of the sensor or where you have determined the leak is. While your machine is still under vacuum, fill the dam or funnel with the recommended epoxy or silicone and release the vacuum slowly. This will pull the sealant into the leak. Let the sealant cure for an extended period. Follow dry time instructions of the product you are using.

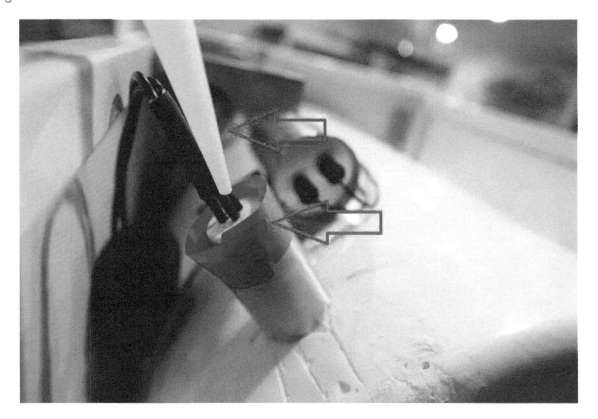

Fingers crossed for you. This can be extremely frustrating, especially if you just purchased your freeze dryer or are in the middle of a freeze dry cycle. I have heard that if you are scheduling an appointment with Harvestright for help with diagnosis, set up an ongoing appointment (for the next day or the soonest available) before you even talk to a person. That way you are not drawing out the troubleshooting and diagnosis. The longer it takes for them to get back to you or you go on with your life for a few days, the tougher it is to remember where you left off or what happened on the last phone call or email. I have also had good results with positivity (not just for Harvest Right). If you call into customer service with a bad attitude or showing discouragement, you will get an equal reaction. If your attitude is one willing to learn and experiment, most of the people I have dealt with at HR love these machines and take pride in their work and product.

My gratitude for freeze dryers!

I want to take this opportunity to thank all freeze dryers who have supported our Youtube, Social media groups and freeze drying resources by purchasing this book or products from us. We have been so proud to be able to help individuals as well as build this amazing freeze drying community with the help of all of you. The amount of knowledge and kindness given will never go unnoticed. Our groups and reach have grown way beyond our wildest dreams and that is 100% because of freeze dryers like you!

We wish you all the best in your freeze drying ventures.

HAPPY FREEZE DRYING!

Made in the USA
Las Vegas, NV
22 October 2023

79512981R00092